# NEEDLEPOINT
Techniques and Projects

# NEEDLEPOINT
## Techniques and Projects

Jenni Kirkham

Kangaroo Press

This book is dedicated to my parents:
the late S.W. (Bill) Smith
—designer, builder and flyer of model planes—
and
Olive Smith
—embroiderer, dressmaker, cook and gardener—
who taught me most of the skills I needed to
write this book

**Acknowledgments**
I would like to thank several people for their help while I wrote this book:
• Steve and Dawn of Busy Beaver Photos in Balcatta, WA, for their help and advice, loan of equipment and patience as I monopolised their photocopier for long periods
• Howard Bellamy, for applying his skills in food photography to the field of embroidery, with the outstanding results which illustrate this book
• My family, Gordon, Gail and Sarah, who have coped with a degree of chaos greater than any they have suffered previously as everything gave way to the book
• Thanks also to Lorraine McGinnis, who gave me the idea, Vivienne Garforth, who nagged me to get on with it, and all my other friends who believed I could do it.

First published in 1992 by Kangaroo Press Pty Ltd
3 Whitehall Road (P.O. Box 75) Kenthurst 2156
Typeset by G.T. Setters Pty Limited
Printed in Hong Kong by Colorcraft Ltd

ISBN 0 86417 438 X

# Contents

Project 9: Apple blossom cushion

# Introduction

Needlepoint, the widely accepted name for the technique of embroidering on canvas, is gaining in popularity in Australia, mirroring trends overseas, particularly in Britain and the United States, where several companies have established thriving businesses designing patterns and marketing kits and materials.

Many embroiderers start canvas embroidery with a 'tapestry'. Widely available, tapestry canvases are either printed with coloured pictures or 'trammed' with horizontal lines of coloured wools to build up the design. These are then entirely covered in rows of tent stitch. A variety of different subjects enables this type of work to be used for the upholstery of chairs and stools, for practical articles such as bags and cushions, and as framed pictures purely for decoration. In recent years Semco's excellent longstitch kits have become very popular. The design outline is printed in black on the white canvas, and filled in with long straight stitches embellished with a small amount of surface stitchery in the final stages. While very quick to work, the technique is mainly restricted to pictures, due to the lengths of the stitches.

Needlepoint follows on from these techniques, adding to the basic repertoire of tent and satin stitches with a range of decorative and textural stitches, exploring and exploiting the geometric qualities of the basic canvas. Designs usually start at a central point and are developed by counting threads, following a chart or graph. The results are colourful and hardwearing, and can be applied to a wide range of personal and household items. Most designs are fairly quickly worked, making smaller items in particular extremely suitable for gifts, as they are also light in weight and easy to pack and post.

This book aims to teach the beginner, and those already experienced in tapestry or longstitch, the fascinating craft of needlepoint canvas work. As well, it provides a wide range of patterns to appeal to the more expert embroiderer who is always on the lookout for 'something a bit different'.

Project 8: Victorian pincushion 'Peace'

# The traditions of needlepoint

While embroidery on canvas was not commonly used for domestic items until the sixteenth century, there is evidence to suggest that the craft dates back to Roman times. The ground fabric then was probably a very fine evenweave linen rather than a stiffened canvas. The technique survived the Dark Ages to flourish in Church embroidery at the time of the Norman conquest of Britain. Over the next few hundred years, *opus anglicanum*, which incorporated jewels and precious metal threads, became prized throughout Christendom; several surviving examples show the use of canvas embroidery. *Opus anglicanum* was the work of professional embroiderers, who served a seven-year apprenticeship before they qualified. The Black Death, which wiped out a huge proportion of the European population in the middle of the fourteenth century, together with the uncertainties of the Hundred Years' War, saw the end of the great era of Church embroidery, and it was not until the more settled times of the later Tudor period that the craft was again revived.

With this time of comparative peace came greater prosperity. Great houses were built by the nobility; their ladies began to make these new domains more comfortable by embroidering hangings and long cushions, and smaller personal items such as bookcovers and workbags. They discovered that a variation of tent stitch could produce an effect very like the weave of the newly fashionable and very expensive tapestries being produced in France and Belgium. Even today we call that branch of canvas embroidery 'tapestry', although the term is more correctly applied to a woven fabric. Professional embroiderers once more found a niche, as employees in the noble households. Their job was to design the projects and advise their ladies on stitches and colours. They took their patterns from the wealth of illustrated books just becoming available as printing became established, as well as from the herbs and fragrant plants grown in the gardens of the time, and stitched them in wools, silks and metal threads.

As overseas trade increased during the following centuries, the influences of Middle Eastern and Oriental design were seen in the needlework produced. More decorative embroidery was worked, with tent stitch pictures of royalty, other portraits and Biblical scenes being very popular. Some furniture was upholstered, and crewel work began to replace canvas work in popularity. The first samplers were produced around this time, more often as a type of pattern reference than the child's introduction to embroidery that they became in Victorian times.

Canvas embroidery saw a revival in the eighteenth century, as the beginnings of the industrial revolution created a newly affluent middle class. They constructed elegant town houses and furnished them comfortably with curtains and carpets, upholstered furniture, and all kinds of accessories like firescreens and cushions. The first craft shops were established at this time, selling fabrics, patterns, and even kits. After the French Revolution, however, when Napoleon's new order ushered in the trend to neo-classicism, embroidery was thought of as homely and unsophisticated, and once more waned in popularity.

As the industrial revolution gathered momentum, canvas similar to the modern product began to be mass produced. When, in the late 1850s, the first chemically based dyes were developed, the stage was set for another revival of canvas work. In Germany, an enterprising printer started to produce patterns and pictures as graphs, at first coloured in by hand, and later, as the craft of printing progressed, produced in brilliant colours to match the new Berlin wools.

Berlin woolwork became a craze among Victorian needleworkers. They produced a huge range of items for personal and household use and adornment, with subjects ranging from flowers and fruit through soulful dogs on cushions to portraits and copies of famous paintings, mostly in wool on canvas, sometimes with silk threads and glass beads. The standards of design were much criticised, leading William Morris and his associates to return to the influences of the seventeenth century crewel patterns when they turned their attentions to textiles in the latter decades of the nineteenth century. As their influence began to be felt in all aspects of architecture and interior design, Berlin woolwork decreased in popularity.

The early part of this century saw little interest in canvas work other than a brief revival in the 1930s by members of the Bloomsbury Group of artists, who felt that embroidery had a valid place in the decorative arts. Today kits and canvases are readily available in department stores and craft shops. Manufacturers have been constantly improving the quality of their wools and canvases, and they have produced new threads as synthetic fibres have developed. History has shown us that canvaswork articles are very durable, so the materials are now designed to be lightfast and insectproof, with the life expectancy of several hundred years demanded by professional contemporary embroiderers.

We now have a wide variety of materials to work with, and a firmly established tradition on which to build. Today's canvas embroidery designs incorporate many traditional stitches and techniques, but there is a growing tendency to mix surface stitchery not usually associated with evenweave fabrics, and a growing awareness that the basic canvas weave can be decorative in itself, and does not always need to be covered completely. Contemporary creative embroiderers are exploiting colours and textures, pattern and form, in ways that elevate the craft to an art form and, through classes and workshops organised by the various embroidery guilds throughout the world, they are passing on their ideas and skills to those less experienced, thus keeping the traditions of canvas work growing.

# Materials and equipment

## Canvas

A specialist embroidery shop may offer the needleworker around twenty different canvases, ranging from rug canvas with three holes per 2.5 cm to fine silk gauze with 40 holes per 2.5 cm. However, the average craft shop stocks only the most popular types, and it is these which are used for most of the patterns in this book.

The most useful canvas is white interlock with 12 holes per 2.5 cm. The threads are woven in such a way as to prevent movement, providing a useful counter to the perennial problem of distortion when using diagonal stitches. While the rigidity can be a disadvantage when working eyelets and other pulled thread stitches, the general stability of this type of canvas makes it ideal for beginners.

Penelope canvas has 10 holes per 2.5 cm and is available in either white or beige shades. It has a characteristic weave consisting of pairs of threads in each direction, and is the traditional 'tapestry' canvas. It is most useful for basic stitches like tent and cross, rather than for textural work which tends not to cover the threads evenly.

Plastic canvas is a modern innovation, rather strange to use at first, but it has the advantage of being non-fraying, suitable for cutting into various shapes, and because of its rigidity it does not need to be mounted on a frame before being worked. It is also washable (unlike woven canvas), extremely durable, and can be built into three dimensional forms. It is available with either 7 or 10 holes per 2.5 cm, and in addition to rectangular sheets, is also produced in a variety of shapes which are designed for making boxes. The coarser mesh, 7 holes per 2.5 cm, is also available in a range of pastel colours. When stitching on plastic canvas, care should be taken that the wrong side is as neat as possible, as it is often visible in the finished item.

Fine silk gauze, while strictly a specialist fabric, is useful for jewellery items; because the threads are closely woven, detailed designs can be worked using fine threads such as a single strand of silk or stranded cotton. Fine evenweave fabric such as Lugano, with 26 threads per 2.5 cm, can be substituted, and is easier to obtain.

Perforated paper is a recent revival of a Victorian craze which, although new to the Australian market, has been available in the United States and Britain for some years. It has a smoother surface on its right side and is fairly strong, although it should be handled with some care to avoid tearing or creasing, especially during unpicking. Although usually used for cross stitch, it is eminently suitable as a background for needlepoint, especially the diagonal stitches, and can be trimmed into fancy shapes after the embroidery is completed. Available in a range of colours, including gold, the paper itself is a feature of the work; design details only are stitched, with no background filling stitches.

Because creases in canvas can spoil the finished embroidery, it is recommended that canvas be stored rolled around a cardboard tube. Smaller pieces, gauze and perforated paper are best kept flat between two pieces of cardboard until needed.

## Frames

Needlepoint is best worked on a square or rectangular frame in order to maintain the tension required for most stitches.

A slate frame consists of two rollers with a length of webbing tape attached to each, and two side bars. The canvas is sewn to the webbing, then the four pieces are slotted together and held tightly with bolts and wing nuts. Since the advent of the long stitch technique, this type of frame has been easy to obtain. The basic size can be changed by making a spare pair of longer sides, a project most amateur woodworkers find extremely simple.

The most basic frame of all is again an easy woodwork project. The four sides are cut from pine 20 × 45 mm thick and joined with half-lap joints at each corner, glued and pinned. The canvas is fixed in place with drawing pins prior to working.

Commercially produced slate frame

# A guide to canvases

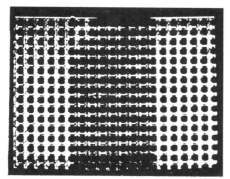

Plastic canvas
10 holes per 2.5 cm

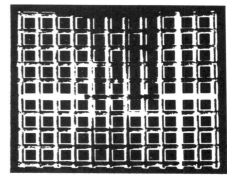

Plastic canvas
7 holes per 2.5 cm

Penelope canvas (double thread canvas)
10 holes per 2.5 cm

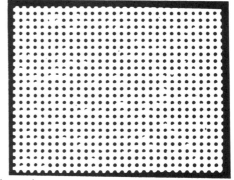

Perforated paper
14 holes per 2.5 cm

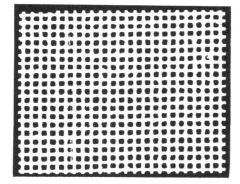

Interlock canvas
12 holes per 2.5 cm

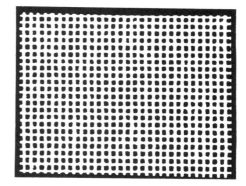

Interlock canvas
14 holes per 2.5 cm

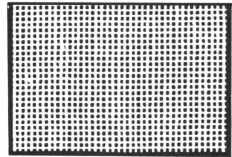

Mono canvas
18 holes per 2.5 cm

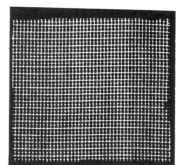

Silk gauze
30 holes per 2.5 cm

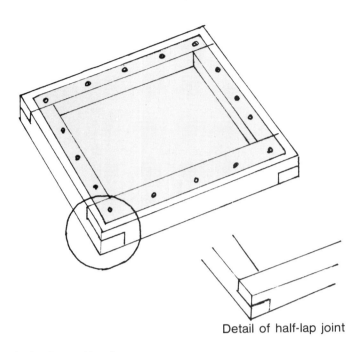

Detail of half-lap joint

A simple working frame

## Threads

Wool is the most natural choice for needlepoint, although it is combined with a variety of other threads in the projects. Standard tapestry wool is colourfast and hard wearing, but a little thick for smaller stitches on size 12 canvas, so my preference is for crewel wool. This comes in pre-cut lengths of 2 ply strands. Usually three strands are sufficient to cover the canvas well, but on a large border of satin stitch, adding a fourth thread gives a better result. The colours are softer and more subtle than those available in tapestry wool, and the shades are closer together.

Metallic threads should be chosen with care. Some are constructed by winding the metallic thread around an inner core of cotton strands, and generally the roughness of the canvas will wear this type of thread to shreds very quickly as you work with it. Much easier to use are the yarns in which the metallic thread is knitted with a nylon filament, such as those produced for knitting and crochet. Thinner threads may be used double to give good coverage of the canvas.

Stranded, soft embroidery and pearl cottons can also be used in needlepoint, and are best worked on the finer canvases and perforated paper if used by themselves.

## Needles

Tapestry needles are thick and blunt with large eyes. They are sold in mixed packets which are ideal for the beginner. Choose a medium thickness, e.g. size 20 for general work on size 12 canvas, and a thinner one for finer canvas. The needle, fully threaded, should pass comfortably through the holes of the canvas without sticking, otherwise the constant pulling needed to make the stitches will cause sore fingers and distort the threads of the canvas. On perforated paper a fine needle is required; it should pass easily through the holes without tearing the background when threaded with a full six strands of cotton.

In addition to tapestry needles, you will need a sharp pointed darning needle for sewing canvas onto a slate frame; and for any of the projects using fine beads a specially designed beading needle will be easier to use than a conventional sewing needle because it has a much thinner eye and can pass through the tiniest beads.

## Other equipment

**Scissors:** One pair to cut canvas, one pair to clip threads.
**Masking tape:** Used to bind raw edges of canvas; 2.5 cm is a good width to buy.
**Strong thread:** Button thread or upholsterers' linen thread for sewing canvas onto working frames.
**Sewing cotton:** For beadwork and making up projects. For added strength, run each length through beeswax before use.
**Marker pens:** Never use any marking pen until you have tested it on a spare piece of the canvas to be worked. It must be totally waterproof or it will bleed into the wools. By far the best marking method is a fadeout pen, which can be used heavily if necessary and will take several days to disappear, a period usually long enough to see most designs well established, if not completed.

# Techniques

## Preparing to work

Cut the canvas to the size specified in the instructions for the chosen project. Run a length of masking tape along one edge, folding it in half to enclose the raw edges, and repeat on the remaining three sides of the canvas. Mark the centre of each side on the masking tape using a pencil.

If using a simple wooden frame, measure and mark the centre points of each side, then place the canvas on top of the frame, aligning the centre markings on the edges with the marks on the frame. Hold in place with a drawing pin at each point, pulling the canvas as tight as possible between them. Next, pull the corners of the canvas into place and pin those firmly. Add more pins halfway between the first, and continue to pin until the canvas is held tightly all round. Hammer the drawing pins down to stop them working loose during stitching.

Before using a slate frame for the first time, mark a permanent line on each webbing tape at the exact centre of each roller. Thread a darning needle with strong thread and knot one end. Turn over the top 1 cm of canvas to the wrong side and place the right side of the webbing tape on the roller along the fold, matching the centre lines on both fabrics. Pin securely in place at the centre and both ends. Starting at the centre, oversew the canvas firmly to the webbing. When the side is reached, finish off the thread securely, then return to the centre and stitch out to the other side. Sew the bottom edge of the canvas in the same way to the second roller, then slot the rollers into the side pieces of the frame. Pull the canvas as tightly as possible across the frame, applying tension by means of the rollers and tightening the wing nuts to hold them in place. Next, take a very long length of thread and, starting with a couple of backstitches at the top corner of the canvas, lace it firmly around the side of the frame, pulling it tightly as you go. Repeat this on the opposite side of the frame. If the canvas becomes slack as work proceeds, tighten it up by adjusting the roller bars and wing nuts and pulling the side lacing more firmly.

## Preparing cotton threads for use

Stranded cotton looks softer and covers the canvas better if it is stripped before use. To do this, cut a working length

of thread, approximately 45 cm long, and separate the six strands completely. Put back together the number of strands required for the project before threading the needle and starting to stitch.

Pearl cotton comes in attractively twisted skeins which can present the beginner with untold problems when it comes to unravelling a working thread. Examine the skein; one end is a single fat loop, the other has two thinner ones. Pull one side of the top loop gently and ease half the skein out of the wrappers; leaving them in place on the remaining skein will enable the colour and thickness of thread to be readily identified. One end of the long skein thus formed will have a knot in the cotton where the two ends have been joined together. Cut through all the loops of thread at that end of the skein. This leaves the entire skein cut into manageable working lengths of thread; to extract one, hold the skein near the paper bands and gently pull one thread out from the top loop. Tie the skein loosely with an overhand knot when not in use to keep it tidy and stop the number bands from slipping off.

## Starting to sew

Most projects start at the centre of the canvas, so mark this point with a fade-out pen, using the markings on the edges of the canvas as a guide.

Threads are easiest to handle and receive less wear during stitching if they are cut no longer than 80 cm. Crewel wool is pre-cut to approximately this length.

To thread the needle, fold the required number of thread strands into a loop about 5 cm from one end, pinching it firmly between thumb and forefinger. Push this loop through the eye of the needle and gently pull it from the other side until the short end pops through.

For the very first stitch on the canvas, tie a knot in the end of the wool. This is the only time a knot is ever used, as once the first stitches are in place every other thread can be joined in by sliding it through the back of them.

Start the work by stabbing the needle down through the canvas about 2 cm away from the centre point, leaving the knot resting on the surface. Work the first stitch or stitches from the chart, and finish off the end of the wool by sliding it through the back of the work, snipping off the surplus thread at the end. When sufficient stitches have been

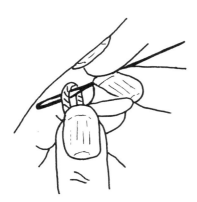

Make a loop of yarn and pull it tight over the needle

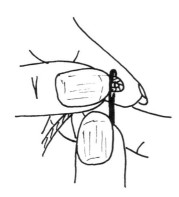

Push the loop through the eye of the needle

worked around the centre point to cover the thread between the knot and the very first stitch, pull the knot upwards away from the canvas and cut the thread close to the surface.

Take care with dark colours in particular when finishing off. It is better to end a leaf, for example, by threading the green thread back through the same leaf, because any fluffy ends carried into a background area of paler colour will tend to be picked up by the lighter threads and show through. Similarly, do not 'jump' threads more than about 2 cm, and when working over a thread which has been carried across a space, try not to split the fibres with the working thread. Wherever possible, try to come up at the start of a stitch

in an empty hole of the canvas, and put the needle down into a hole already occupied with thread.

Finally, a word on comfort. As with all needlework, good daylight provides ideal working conditions, but many of us need to use artificial light. Make sure in that case that the canvas is well lit, and that you adopt a comfortable working position. Frames can be bought with stands, or used resting against the edge of a table or across the arms of a chair when working. Stitching is best done with both hands, one underneath and the other on top, using a stabbing motion with the needle. Take care with chair heights; move around and stretch a little from time to time if sewing for a long period. If you are comfortable, needlepoint can be a relaxing and absorbing pastime.

## How to work from a chart

There are two different types of chart for needlepoint. Projects which use a combination of stitches are drawn with each line of the chart representing a thread of the canvas, while those such as the Victorian style pincushions, which are mainly in tent stitch, are charted with each square on the graph representing one stitch. The instructions for each project show which method is being used.

Most projects start with the centre point, which should be marked on the canvas. Many designs are symmetrical, and for clarity only a portion is charted. The instructions show how to repeat this type of design to complete the project.

Work all the details first and fill in the backgrounds last. If you make a mistake, unpick the wool carefully, pulling the canvas threads as little as possible. Do not re-use unpicked wool as it has usually thinned considerably and will not cover the canvas well enough a second time. Try also to keep the strands of wool as flat as possible, especially on longer straight stitches. Untwist the threads at intervals while you work, and do not pull the stitches too tightly. Ideally, they should rest lightly across the canvas threads without being at all loose.

You may also find it easier to work from a chart by having an enlarged photocopy made, then colouring in the stitch pattern with felt-tipped pens.

# The stitches

## Algerian eye stitch (star stitch)
Each eyelet is composed of eight stitches worked over two threads of canvas into a central hole.

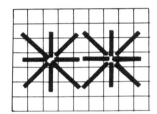

Algerian eye stitch

## Alternating tent stitch (diagonal open ground)
Work in diagonal rows from top right to bottom left. Each new row begins two threads away from the previous one, and the canvas shows between the stitches. When stitching a woven tartan fabric effect, as in the Scottie sampler, alternating tent stitch is worked in straight lines, and the spaces are filled with the background colour.

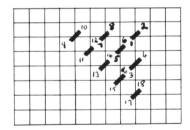

Alternating tent stitch

## Back stitch
Worked in a line in any direction over one or two threads of the canvas, back stitch is used for stems, lettering and other details, as well as being worked to cover bare threads of canvas between other stitches, as seen in the plastic canvas jewellery and Christmas items.

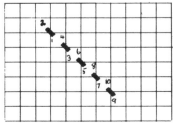

Back stitch

## Basketweave tent stitch
Work in diagonal rows from top right to bottom left over all intersections of the canvas. The stitch takes its name from the pattern made on the back of the work, and is the basic 'tapestry' stitch used on canvas.

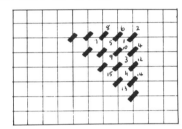

Basketweave tent stitch

## Brick stitch
Straight stitches are worked over four threads in horizontal rows, leaving one hole between each stitch. The second row of stitches is worked between the first, but dropped down two threads. The two-thread gap left at the top is later filled with a row of half-size compensating stitches to make the top edge even. Double and triple brick stitches are worked in the same way, but blocks of two and three stitches respectively are used to build the pattern.

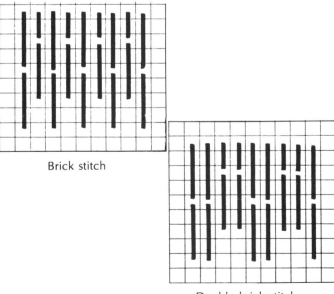

Brick stitch

Double brick stitch

Types of canvas

Commercially produced slate frame

Projects 1, 2 and 3: Pincushion, scissors case and needlecase

Project 6: Victorian pincushion 'Love'

## Buttonhole stitch

Usually not associated with canvas stitchery, buttonhole stitch is very useful on plastic canvas for finishing the edges neatly. Working with the edge nearest to you, from left to right, make one stitch in each hole, keeping the thread under the needle to produce the characteristic looped edge.

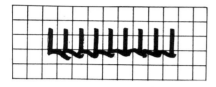

Buttonhole stitch

## Chain stitch

Another stitch more usually found in traditional embroidery, chain stitch can be worked on canvas over one or two threads, in any direction, and makes a useful filling or border stitch. Work it by bringing the needle out at the start of the line. Make a loop, insert the needle at the same point, and bring it out in the next hole of the canvas and up through the loop. Each stitch begins and ends in the previous loop, moving one thread along the canvas each time.

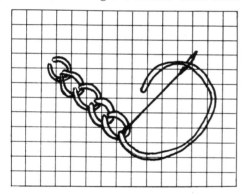

Chain stitch

## Chequer stitch

A composite stitch consisting of squares of satin stitch worked diagonally over 1, 2, 3, 2 and 1 threads, alternating with squares composed of three rows of three tent stitches.

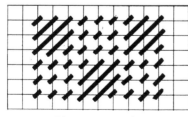

Chequer stitch

## Couching

More often seen in traditional embroidery, couching is a method usually used to secure a decorative thread to the background fabric, especially when it is too thick to be used in conventional stitchery. On the cover of the jewel case,

gold Ribbon Floss is held flat against the surface of the canvas with groups of three tent stitches. Couched threads can be sewn down with many different stitches, including straight stitch, cross stitch and herringbone, all of which can be readily adapted to the canvas by working one stitch into each hole.

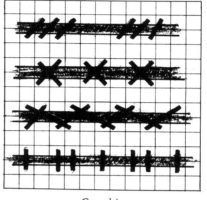

1. Using tent stitch

2. Using cross stitch

3. Using herringbone

4. Using straight stitch

Couching

## Cross stitch

This traditional canvaswork stitch is worked over one or two threads. There are two methods: either make each cross individually, working the first arm of the stitch from bottom right to top left and the other arm from bottom left to top right, or work a row of cross stitches by embroidering the first stitches in a line from left to right, then working back in the opposite direction to complete the row. Whichever method is used, the top stitches must all lie in the same direction.

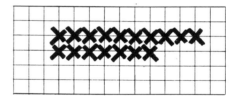

Cross stitch

## Cushion stitch

A simple but effective stitch which uses satin stitch blocks consisting of diagonal stitches over 1, 2, 3, 2 and 1 threads. Alternate blocks are worked in opposite directions, and the pattern is very striking when worked in contrasting colours.

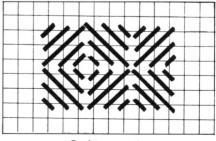

Cushion stitch

## Diamond eyelet stitch

Start with a vertical straight stitch over four threads into the centre hole and move in a clockwise direction. The tops of the next three stitches are one hole down and to the right of the preceding one, and all enter the central hole. When the horizontal stitch over four threads is made, the next four stitches move one hole down and one hole left. The bottom vertical stitch signals a change of direction for the third quarter of the eyelet, which moves one hole left and one hole up, and the final three stitches are taken one hole to the right and one hole up to meet the first stitch again.

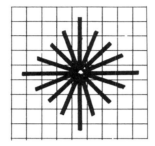

Diamond eyelet

## Double cross stitch

This consists of an upright cross stitch made over four threads of the canvas, with a diagonal cross stitch over two threads worked on top of it.

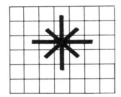

Double cross stitch

## French knots

Another traditional stitch which has been adapted to canvas work, this is perhaps not so easy to work on such a rigid background, especially with the stab-stitch sewing action. Bring the needle out at the lower left hole, as if making a tent stitch, then wind the thread twice around it. Turn the needle clockwise and insert it through the upper right hole. Hold the loops firmly while pulling the thread through.

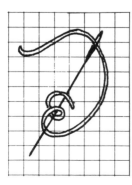

Step 1

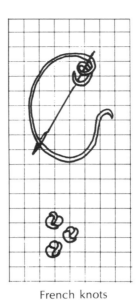

Step 2

Finished stitches

French knots

## Horizontal Van Dyke

Usually used as a filling stitch in vertical rows, this version of Van Dyke stitch has been used on the perforated paper photo frame mat to give a solid narrow block of colour. Each cross stitch is two threads high and four threads long, and overlaps the preceding stitch by two threads.

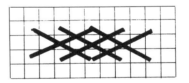

Horizontal Van Dyke stitch

## Hungarian stitch

This filling stitch consists of groups of three straight stitches over 2, 4 and 2 threads of the canvas. One hole is left between each group of stitches on the first row; the second row interlocks, with the long stitches occupying the empty holes. To make the top and sides of the stitched area straight, compensating stitches are worked over 1 or 2 threads as shown in the diagram.

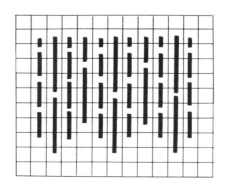

## Lazy daisy loops (detached chain stitch)

Yet another traditional embroidery stitch which has proved easy to transpose to canvas stitchery. It is worked in the same way as chain stitch, with the thread looped around and the needle inserted into the starting hole, but after the needle is brought out through the loop, it goes down into the next hole, making a small straight stitch which anchors the loop in position. A double version of the stitch is used on the jewel case, where a stitch over 2 intersections of the canvas shares the same starting hole as one over 3 threads.

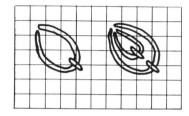

Lazy daisy loops

## Leaf stitch

Although worked as individual leaves in the flower patterns throughout this book, leaf stitch can also be stitched in rows to form a textured ground. Work up one side and down the other on each leaf of the pattern in turn, and fit the second row between the first as shown in the diagram.

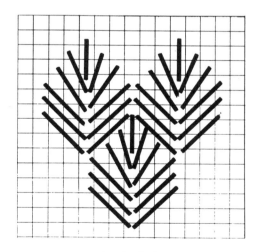

Leaf stitch

## Milanese stitch

Work diagonal stitches over 1, 2, 3 and 4 intersections, covering the area to be filled with diagonal lines. The second row is worked over 4, 3, 2 and 1 threads in turn so that it interlocks neatly with the first. Fill the edge spaces with compensating stitches as shown.

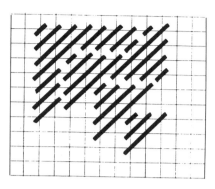

Milanese stitch

## Mosaic stitch

A simple stitch composed of groups of three diagonal stitches worked over 1, 2 and 1 threads of canvas, forming a small square block pattern. It looks very attractive when worked in two colours.

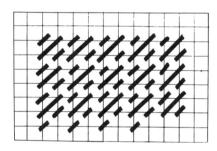

Mosaic stitch

## Parisian stitch

Work straight stitches over 2 then 4 threads across the canvas. The following rows interlock, with the long stitches worked beneath the short ones of the previous row.

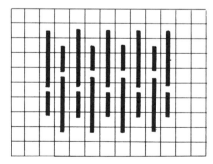

Parisian stitch

21

## Reversed tent stitch (knitting stitch)

Worked in vertical rows, the lines of tent stitch slope in opposite directions on alternate rows, making a ground pattern which looks like knitted stocking stitch.

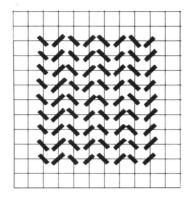

Reversed tent stitch

## Rice stitch (crossed corners)

A striking border stitch which also makes an effective filler for large areas, rice stitch can be worked in one or two colours. The first part of the stitch is a large diagonal cross over 4 threads. Each arm in turn is then crossed with a diagonal stitch over 2 threads in a contrasting colour.

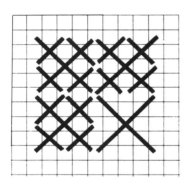

Rice stitch

## Roumanian leaf stitch

Each leaf consists of a straight stitch over two threads followed by six horizontal straight stitches from points A to B, each couched down with a small straight stitch in the centre.

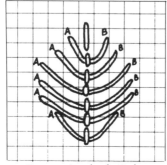

Roumanian leaf stitch

## Satin stitch (straight stitch, long stitch)

Satin stitch is a term used throughout the patterns in the book to denote a group of straight stitches which do not fall into any definite stitch category. Individual charts show how these are used, and the lengths of the stitches required in any given area. For practical purposes, it is usually worked over 4 threads or less, but in the long stitch variation, used mainly for pictorial subjects, the stitches are often much longer.

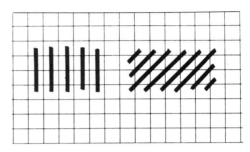

Satin stitch

## Slanted Gobelin stitch

Diagonal stitches are worked in rows over two threads of canvas. A long tramming stitch can be taken first across the middle holes to be covered by the stitches, providing extra padding as the stitch is worked.

without tramming

with tramming

Slanted Gobelin stitch

## Smyrna cross stitch

This is constructed with a large diagonal cross stitch over four threads of canvas with an upright cross stitch over four threads worked on top. Care should be taken that all the stitches cross in the same direction throughout a project.

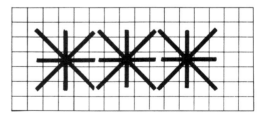

Smyrna cross stitch

## Tent stitch

The basic 'tapestry' stitch, tent stitch should not be confused with half cross stitch, which looks the same on the front of the work, but has a straight stitch on the back of the canvas. Tent stitch has a long diagonal stitch on the back and uses more wool than half cross, but it is so much more durable that it is essential to use it for items which will be subjected to wear. Lines of tent stitch can be worked in any direction, but for filling large areas of canvas it is best to use the basketweave variation.

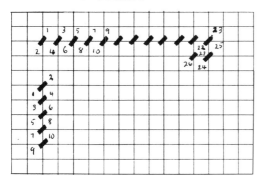

Tent stitch

## Trammed cross stitch
Tram the area to be worked by taking a long stitch from one side to the other across the centre row of holes to be covered by the stitches. Work back over this stitch with a row of cross stitches over two threads of the canvas. Make sure that the top stitches of all the crosses lie in the same direction.

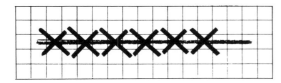

Trammed cross stitch

## Trammed Gobelin stitch
Take a long stitch from one side of the working area to the other across the middle row of holes to be covered by the Gobelin stitch. Work back over this stitch with straight stitches over two threads of canvas.

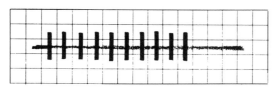

Trammed Gobelin stitch

## Triple oblong cross
A composite stitch consisting of a horizontal oblong cross stitch six threads long and one thread high, topped with a vertical oblong cross stitch three threads high and two threads wide, and a horizontal oblong cross stitch two threads long and one thread in height.

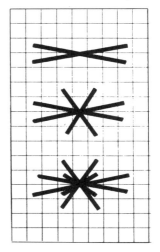

Triple oblong cross

## Upright cross stitch
This stitch can be worked singly or in rows in the same way as ordinary cross stitch. The stitch is usually worked over either one or two threads of the canvas. Care must be taken to make sure that all the top stitches of the crosses lie in the same direction.

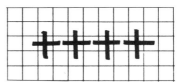

Upright cross stitch

# The projects

# 1. Pincushion

*Materials*
canvas, 12 holes per 2.5 cm, 17 cm square
Appleton's Crewel Wool, 1 hank each of

| | | | |
|---|---|---|---|
| yellow | 472 | green | 341 |
| light pink | 752 | beige | 701 |
| dark pink | 753 | | |

pink velvet, 17 cm square
matching sewing cotton
filling material (soft toy filling, bran, sawdust or cut-up
stockings)

**1.** Mark the centre point of the canvas and start the embroidery with a cross stitch over two diagonal threads in yellow. Note that each line of the graph represents one thread of the canvas. Following the chart, work the central flower in satin stitches around the central cross stitch, and then the back stitch stems in green. Finish the motif by working the leaves as shown. Use three strands of wool throughout.

**2.** After completing the flowers and leaves, count two threads diagonally from the tip of the last leaf and work the cross stitch border in light pink.

**3.** Following the chart closely, fill in the background with brick stitch in beige, starting at the outer edges of the design and working in towards the centre. Note that in order to fit around the flower and leaf shapes, some of the stitches are shorter than the normal four threads. These are called 'compensating stitches'.

**4.** Complete the design with two rows of tent stitch around the edge in dark pink.

**5.** Make up the pincushion by placing the worked canvas face down on the right side of the velvet square. Stitch around the edge, right up to the outer line of tent stitch, leaving an opening in one side. Trim borders to approximately 1 cm wide, and cut diagonally across the corners to remove excess fabric, taking care not to cut into any of the stitching. Turn through, and gently push corners into shape. Fill pincushion with chosen filling, turn in raw edges along opening and pin. Using matching sewing thread doubled, slip stitch in place.

## Making up

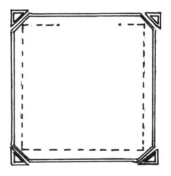

Seam together the canvas and backing fabric. Clip corners

Turn through to right side and stuff firmly

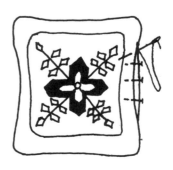

Pin opening and slip stitch together

24

## Working chart for pincushion

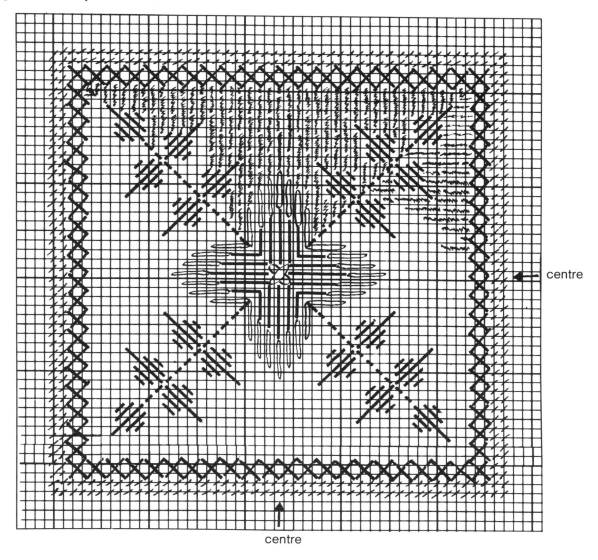

centre

centre

(each line on the graph represents one thread of canvas)

**Key**

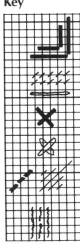

Satin stitch (light pink 752)

Tent stitch (dark pink 753)
Satin stitch (dark pink 753)

Cross stitch (light pink 752)

Cross stitch (yellow 472)

Back stitch (green 341)
Satin stitch (green 341)

Brick stitch (beige 701)

# 2. Scissors case

*Materials*
canvas, 12 holes per 2.5 cm, 15 cm square
Appleton's Crewel Wool, 1 hank each of

| | | | |
|---|---|---|---|
| yellow | 472 | green | 341 |
| light pink | 752 | beige | 701 |
| dark pink | 753 | | |

velvet, 11 × 13 cm
lightweight card, 11 × 13 cm
beige sewing cotton
40 cm cord to go around edge
felt, 11 × 13 cm

**1.** Measure the canvas and draw a line 7 cm down from the top. Measure in 8 cm from the left hand side and mark the point where the lines intersect. This is the position of the yellow cross stitch at the centre of the flower. Follow the chart, on which each line represents a thread of the canvas, and work the cross stitch over two threads. Join in the light pink wool and work the satin stitch petals around the centre. Complete the flower with dark pink satin stitches, and work a stem of 14 back stitches in green from the bottom left hand side of the flower motif. Finish with two pairs of satin stitch leaves as shown on the chart.
**2.** Trace the template from the diagram onto a piece of greaseproof paper and cut it out. Place it on top of the embroidery, lining the cross up with the yellow cross stitch in the needlepoint. Draw a line on the canvas around the edge of the template.
**3.** Fill in the area within the marked lines with rows of brick stitch in beige, using the chart as a guide to their placement.
**4.** When the work is complete, cut two pieces each from the card and the felt, using the template. Cover one piece of card with velvet, glueing down the long edges first, and then the top and bottom. Trim the corners of the fabric to eliminate bulk. Cover the second piece in the same way with the embroidered canvas, taking care that no canvas shows around the edges.

**5.** Cut two pieces of felt using the template, and glue each to the back of one of the covered card shapes. Place the two pieces of the scissors case together with the felt covered sides facing. Using beige sewing cotton doubled for extra strength, oversew them firmly together. Start at the top corner, sew down one long side, across the bottom and up the other side. Finish off securely.
**6.** Sew on cord to cover the seams; start at the top corner, sew down one long side, across the bottom and up to the top of the second side. Then stitch the cord in place around the top edge, finishing at the same point at which you started. Cut the cord ends to 5 cm, tease out the individual strands, then darn each one in turn into the cord edging to finish off.

**Key**

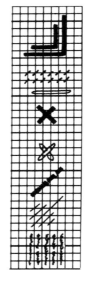

Satin stitch (light pink 752)

Tent stitch (dark pink 753)
Satin stitch (dark pink 753)

Cross stitch (light pink 752)

Cross stitch (yellow 472)

Back stitch (green 341)

Satin stitch (green 341)

Brick stitch (beige 701)

# Working chart for scissors case

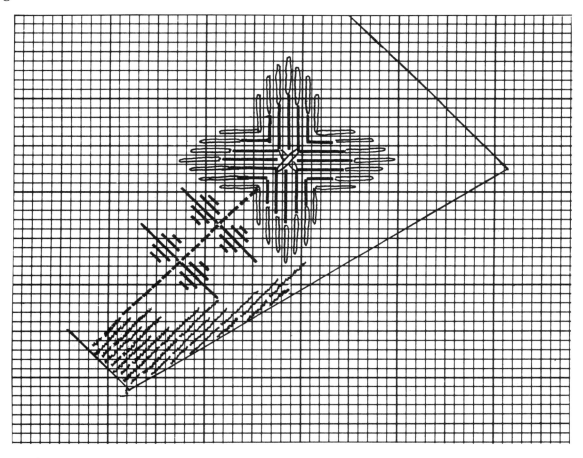

(each line on the graph represents one thread of canvas)

## Making up

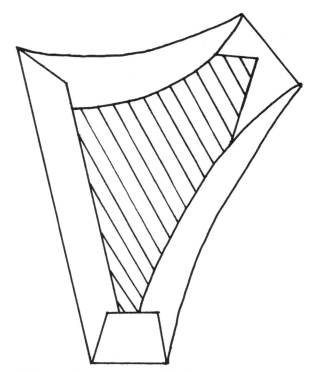

Scissors case template

Glue the fabric turnings over the card, clipping corners

# 3. Needlecase

*Materials*
canvas, 12 holes per 2.5 cm, 15 × 27cm
lining taffeta, 15 × 27 cm
curtain tie-back stiffening, 15 × 27 cm
felt, 17 cm square
Appleton's Crewel Wool, 1 hank each of

| | | | |
|---|---|---|---|
| yellow | 472 | green | 341 |
| light pink | 752 | beige | 701 |
| dark pink | 753 | | |

matching sewing cotton

**1.** Measure down 7 cm from the long edge of the canvas and 7.5 cm in from the left hand side to find the starting point. Work yellow cross stitch over two diagonal threads in this position, following the chart. Each line on the graph represents one thread of the canvas. Use three strands of wool.
**2.** Continue to work design, following the stitches and colours shown on the chart. After completing the flower motif work the stems and leaves in green wool.
**3.** Count out one thread from the tip of the leaf on the left hand side and, using light pink wool, work cross stitch border around motif.
**4.** Fill in background with brick stitch in beige wool. Using dark pink, work two rows of tent stitch around the top, the left side and the bottom of the motif, and five rows at the right hand side for the spine area of the needlecase.
**5.** Work the back section of the needlecase in linear cross stitch, 23 stitches × 23 rows.
**6.** To make up the needlecase, pin the lining fabric to the embroidered canvas, right sides facing, then pin the stiffening on top. Turn the work over and stitch securely around the edge of the embroidery, leaving a 5 cm opening along the cross stitched edge.
**7.** Trim the stiffening close to the stitching, then trim the canvas and lining edges to about 1 cm in width, cutting the corners diagonally to minimise bulkiness. Turn through to the right side, easing the corners out gently, then press lightly. Tuck in the raw edges of the opening and pin

together. Using matching sewing cotton, close the opening with slip stitch.
**8.** Cut the square of felt in half and trim the edges of the pieces with pinking shears. Place on the lined side of the cover and test for fit by folding all layers in half. The felt should not protrude from the cover; if it does, trim off a little bit more. Backstitch the felt in place down the centre of the needlecase, using matching sewing cotton. Work through the layers of felt, the lining and the stiffening only.
**9.** Complete the needlecase with plaited tie ends. Use one length of wool in each of three colours, and thread these strands through a few of the canvas threads at the edge of the embroidery. Remove the needle and level the ends. Separate the strands into the three separate colours and braid them together for about 12 cm. Finish with an overhand knot and trim the ends to form a small tassel. Repeat this procedure for the other edge and close the needlecase by tying the two plaited cords together in a bow.

## Making up

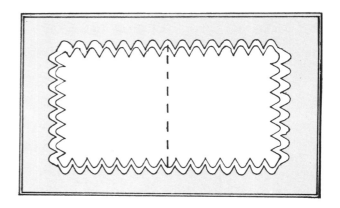

Sewing in the felt pages

## Making a twisted cord

Use two strands each of beige, green and pink tapestry wools, cut three times the length of the finished cord, and tie them together at one end with a firm but not tight overhand knot.

Anchor the knot with a large pin to a firm surface such as the arm of an upholstered chair, or a cushion.

Take the ends of the wool and twist them in a clockwise direction, keeping them under slight tension, until the centre of the twisted thread begins to kink slightly.

Fold the end you are holding up to the knot and ease the knot open enough to enable you to slip the end through the loop. Pull the knot tight, then gently work down the length of the cord, making sure that the twists lie across each other smoothly.

This is also a good way to keep crewel wools tidy when not in use; store them in a cane basket for an attractive decorating feature.

Making the plaited ties

Tying an overhand knot

## Working the set of sewing accessories

If wished, the pincushion, scissors case and needlecase can be worked as a set on one piece of canvas 35 cm square.

Mark out the canvas as shown in the diagram, and when the embroidery has been completed, cut out each piece with 2 cm borders. Make up following the directions given in the individual projects.

The complete needlework set requires only one skein each of the yellow, light pink and green wool, and two skeins each of beige and dark pink.

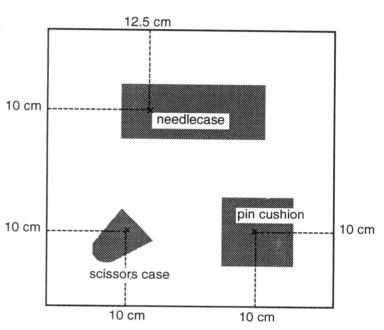

Layout for working complete needlework set on one piece of canvas

## Working chart for needlecase

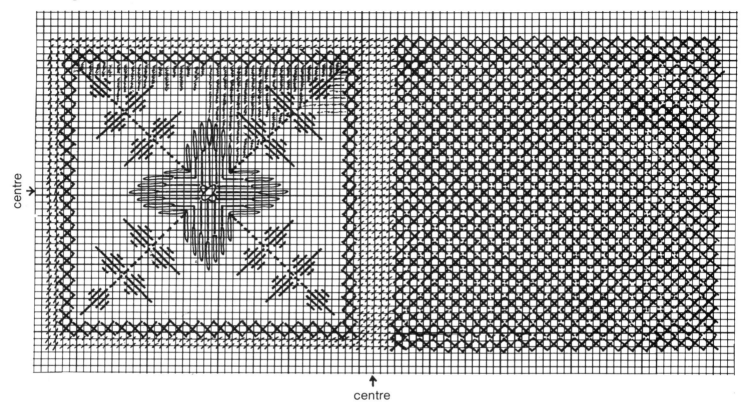

centre

↑
centre

(each line on the graph represents one thread of canvas)

**Key**

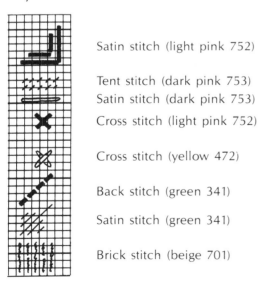

Satin stitch (light pink 752)

Tent stitch (dark pink 753)
Satin stitch (dark pink 753)

Cross stitch (light pink 752)

Cross stitch (yellow 472)

Back stitch (green 341)

Satin stitch (green 341)

Brick stitch (beige 701)

# 4. Eidelweiss cushion

*Materials*
canvas, 14 holes per 2.5 cm, 25 cm square
Appleton's Crewel Wool, 1 hank each of

| | | | |
|---|---|---|---|
| yellow | 472 | pale green | 873 |
| pale pink | 702 | dark green | 245 |
| dark pink | 753 | white | 991 |

2 hanks of
mid green 341

fabric to tone with wool colours, 60 × 115 cm
matching sewing cotton
cushion insert, 35 cm square

**1.** Mark the centre of the canvas. Following chart A, on which each line represents one thread of the canvas, count up two threads from the centre hole and begin the Algerian eye stitch using three strands of yellow wool. Continue to work the design from the graph, turning the canvas 90 degrees clockwise after completing each segment.

**2.** After working the heart and flower motifs of the central area, miss two threads from the outside edge of the white flowers and embroider the tent stitch border in mid green over one thread to define the central square.

**3.** Working from Chart B, continue to work outwards from the centre, one border at a time, using colours and stitches as indicated. For the inner border pattern, make the first cross stitch over two threads directly below the tip of the large green leaf, and count from there to establish the rest of the pattern.

**4.** After completing all the pattern details and borders, fill in the backgrounds in tent stitch using pale green (873) in the inner border, and pale pink (702) in the central square.

**5.** Fold a piece of paper, 12 × 20 cm, in half with the short edges together, and transfer the pattern for the front panels onto it. Cut out around the outside line. Using this pattern, cut four pieces of fabric and mark the large dots on the wrong side of each one.

**6.** Cut two pieces of fabric 39 × 50 cm for the cushion back sections, and two strips 15 cm wide across the width of the fabric for the frill.

**7.** To make up the cushion, pin the mitred strips together to form a square and stitch from the outer edge of each one to the large dot. Backstitch firmly at this point to prevent fraying. Press the seams open and press under the turnings on the inner edges between large dots. Centre this panel over the needlepoint square, easing slightly where necessary to set it right next to the stitching without showing any bare canvas. Tack in place and then stitch into position. This can either be done invisibly on the reverse side, or top stitched close to the fabric edges, by hand or machine. Trim the edges of the canvas panel back to 2 cm all round.

**8.** Seam the two strips for the frill together along the two short sides and trim the selvedges. Press seams flat. Fold the strip in half lengthwise and press the fold. Run a gathering thread along the raw edges and mark the centre points between the seams and the points midway between them.

**9.** Pin the frill all round the cushion top, placing the seams in the centre of two opposite sides, and aligning the marked points evenly with the corners and the centres of the remaining sides. Pull up the gathers evenly and tack the frill in place.

**10.** Fold the two back sections in half to measure 39 × 25 cm, and pin the longer edges to the cushion fronts, covering the frill. Pin the shorter sides in place, overlapping the panels in the centre. Tack everything in place, through all thicknesses. Turn through and check that the frill is evenly distributed around the edge of the cushion and that there are no tucks or puckers, then turn back to the wrong side and sew firmly in place.

**11.** Turn completed cushion cover through to the right side and finish by inserting the cushion pad, taking care to push it firmly into the corners to achieve a good shape.

# Working chart for edelweiss cushion

## Chart A

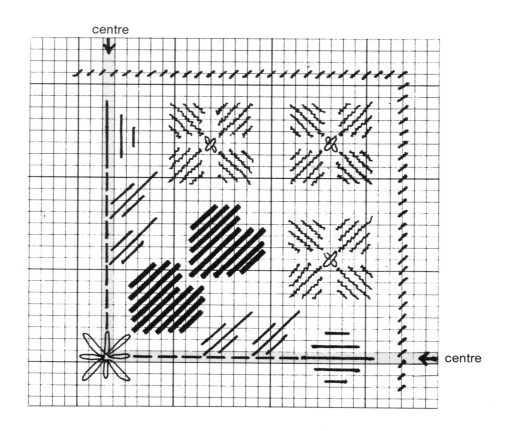

(each line on the graph represents one thread of canvas)

## Key

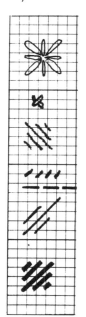

Algerian eye stitch (yellow 472)

Cross stitch (yellow 472)

Satin stitch (white 991)

Tent stitch (mid green 341)
Back stitch (mid green 341)

Satin stitch (mid green 341)

Satin stitch (dark pink 753)

## Key for Chart B (opposite page)

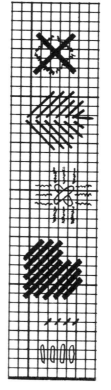

Trammed Gobelin (dark green 245)
Tent stitch (mid green 341)

Heart: satin stitch (dark pink 753)

Flowers: satin stitch (white 991)
Centres: cross stitch (yellow 472)

Leaves: satin stitch (mid green 341)

Rice stitch: cross (dark pink 753)
corners (white 991)

**Chart B**

centre ►

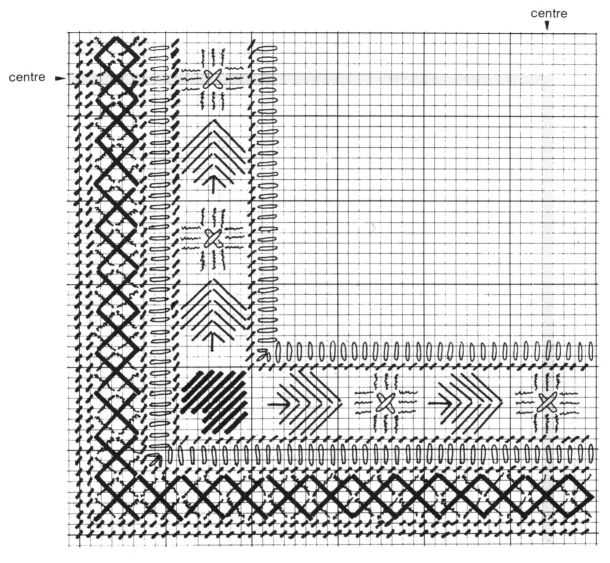

(each line on the graph represents one thread of canvas)

## Making up

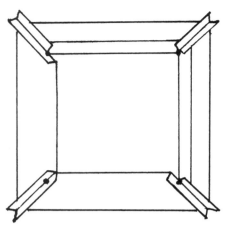

Seam strips together from corners to large dots. Press seam allowances around the centre opening to wrong side.

Pin the frill around the edge of the cushion, matching centre points, and stitch in place, distributing the gathers evenly.

Stitch the back panels of the cushion in place.

Place on fold

Pattern for cushion front panels

Project 4: Edelweiss cushion

Project 5: Forget-me-not box

Project 7: Victorian pincushion 'Joy'

Project 10: Scottie sampler

Project 11: Teddy bear birth sampler

# 5. Forget-me-not box

*Materials*
canvas, 14 holes per 2.5 cm, 25 cm square
Appleton's Crewel Wool, 1 hank each of

| | | | |
|---|---|---|---|
| yellow | 472 | blue | 741 |
| pink | 752 | light blue | 875 |
| pale pink | 877 | green | 401 |

2 hanks of white 991
50 cm white fabric for box sides, 115 cm wide
30 cm lining fabric, 115 cm wide
white poster card
wadding, 20 cm square

**1.** Mark centre point of canvas and start working from the chart with cross stitch over two threads in yellow wool. Each line on the graph represents one thread of canvas. Following the chart, work the central flower in blue, then the green leaves and pink hearts as shown. To complete the octagonal section, miss six threads from the tip of the middle leaf and work cross stitch borders in white.

**2.** Next work the outer border of cross stitch, and fill in the flower and leaf pattern between the two rows and the corner hearts. Fill in the backgrounds of the sections, using tent stitch in light blue for the border of flowers, and alternating tent stitch in pale pink in the central octagon. The corners are also stitched in alternating tent stitch, with the stitches in each one running parallel with the edge of the octagon.

**3.** Complete the square with three rows of cushion stitch and a final border of tent stitch in white.

**4.** To make the box, take the card, fabric and lining material, and cut the following pieces as accurately as possible. Note that the canvas work is not precisely square, and mark pieces A or B in order to avoid confusion.

*From thick white card*
    Base 15.1 × 14.8 cm
    Lid 15.2 (A) × 15 (B) cm
    Side strip 59.8 × 10.8 cm
Score lines across the side strip at intervals of 15.1 cm, 14.8 cm and 15.1 cm.

*From thin white card*
    Lid lining 15.1 (A) × 14.8 (B) cm
    Base lining 14.9 (A) × 14.5 (B) cm
    Side lining strip 58.5 × 10.4 cm

*From white fabric*
    Lid side strip 66 × 15 cm
    Box side strip 64 × 15 cm
    Box base 20 × 20 cm

*From lining fabric*
    Side lining strip 62 × 16.5 cm
    Base lining 20 × 20 cm
    Lid lining 20 × 20 cm

**5.** To make up the box, start by trimming the edges of the canvas around the needlepoint panel to 2 cm and mount it on the thick white card lid section, pulling the edges tightly over the card so that no canvas is visible at the sides. Glue the turnings in place, trimming the corners where necessary to reduce the bulk.

**6.** Press the fabric lid side strip in half lengthways, wrong sides together. Slip the card strip inside the fabric, and keeping one edge to the fold, turn in the seam allowances at each end, glueing them in place on the inside of the shape. Join the short ends with ladder stitch in matching sewing cotton, used double for extra strength. Place the strip around the edges of the needlepoint covered square, folding the card at the corners carefully, and stab pins at intervals of approximately 3 cm all round to hold the two sections together. The raw edges should lie inside, at the back of the square top. Slip stitch the sections together with small stitches, then turn the work over and glue the seam allowances flat against the inside of the lid, clipping into each corner as necessary to reduce the bulk. Complete the lid by lightly glueing a square of wadding to one side of the lid lining section. Cover this in lining fabric, then glue the whole piece to the inside of the box lid.

**7.** Cover the box base card and the side strip in fabric, glueing down the turnings to the wrong side of each piece. Ladder stitch the ends of the side strip together. Pin the base in place and stitch neatly around the edge to hold it in place, removing the pins as you go.

**8.** To line the box, glue wadding to one side of the base lining card then cover it with the square of lining fabric. Cover the side lining strip, glueing the turnings only along one long side and one short one.

**9.** Run a line of glue around the inside top edge of the box. Roll the lining strip lightly with the raw edges of the fabric at the bottom and place inside the box. Gently unroll the strip, and starting at one corner with the unfinished edge of the lining, press it around the edges into the glue, creasing it to fit into each corner in turn. Finish by sticking the finished short edge over the raw edge of the lining at the starting point, tucking in all the top turnings neatly. Lightly glue the bottom turnings to the inside of the box and press the inside base lining piece in place. This does not need to be glued, and should hold the lining tightly in place.

**Working chart for forget-me-not box lid**

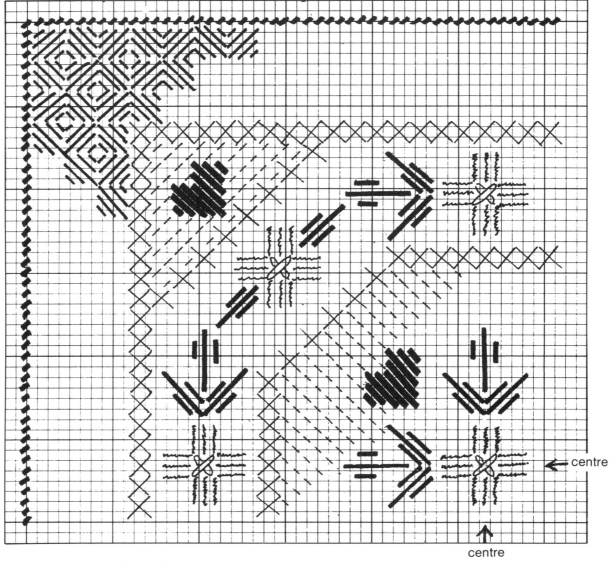

(chart illustrates one quarter of complete pattern)

(each line of the graph represents one thread of canvas)

**Key**

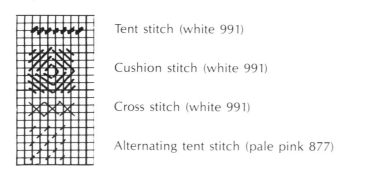

Tent stitch (white 991)

Cushion stitch (white 991)

Cross stitch (white 991)

Alternating tent stitch (pale pink 877)

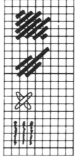

Satin stitch (pink 752)

Satin stitch (green 401)

Cross stitch (yellow 752)

Satin stitch (blue 741)

## Covering the lid and base cards

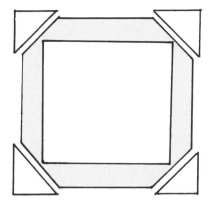

Clip the corners of the fabric.

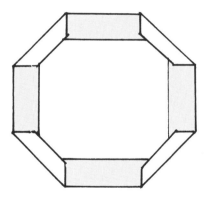

Turn the fabric over the corners of the card.

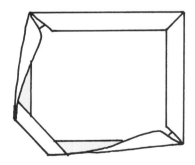

Fold the edge flaps over the card, forming mitred corners.

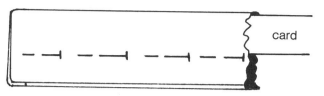

card

Fold the fabric in half and insert the card strip. Turn in the ends and glue the turnings down. Pin card strip in place.

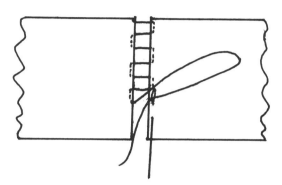

Ladder stitch.

Pin the box lid to the lid side strip.

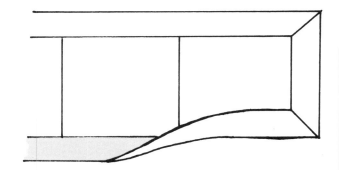

Cover the box side strip with fabric.

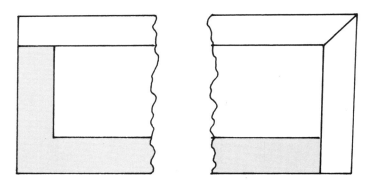

Glue turnings on the lining strip to the top and one short side of the card only.

# Needlepoint with beads

In Victorian times beads were often used in canvas work embroidery, and in some cases stitchery was omitted altogether, the pattern being built up with beads alone. Such work was quite stiff and heavy, and therefore limited in its usefulness. At the same time, fabric pincushions were also being made and decorated by threading beads onto pins, which were then pushed into the cushion to form the designs. Patriotic sentiments printed on scraps of fabric, laces, ribbons and braids were also added in many cases, making the items more suited to decorative than practical use. The designs which follow are based on a combination of these ideas, and an alphabet chart is included so that you can personalise the patterns if you wish.

The beads used for the embroidery are very small seed beads. They are sewn with a doubled length of white sewing cotton, which can be waxed for extra strength by rubbing it across a block of beeswax. A beading needle, which is very fine and has a long, thin eye, is used to work rows of tent stitch. The beading is done first, followed by any other detailed stitchery, and the background is then filled in with tent stitch in crewel wool. The outer borders on each pincushion are of satin stitch, worked with four strands of wool over three threads of canvas. Because the designs are all based on tent stitch, each square on the chart represents one stitch.

Beaded tent stitch

# Charting lettering

## Charting lettering

Use the blank graph paper to copy out the letters for the desired wording. Leave one space between each letter, two between each word. When the graph is complete, count the number of letters and spaces used, then divide by two to find the centre and mark the point with arrows. Match the centre of the charted wording to the centre line of the project chart, and start stitching from that point, working outwards towards each edge.

Occasionally a chart will not fit evenly either side of the centre line of the project graph; in this case another space should be added to the shorter side, either between two letters or two complete words. Put next to a straight letter, e.g. t, l or h, this will not be noticeable; try to avoid putting it after open letters such as c or r or large ones such as m or w, where it may look out of place.

## Charted alphabet

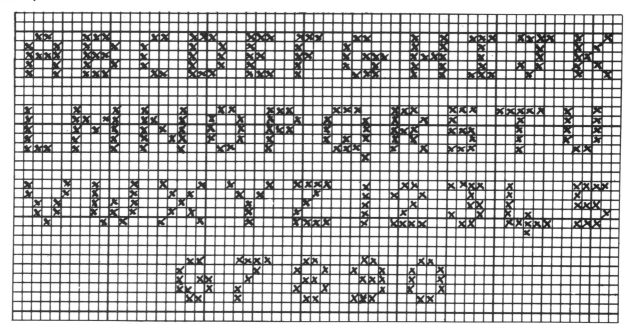

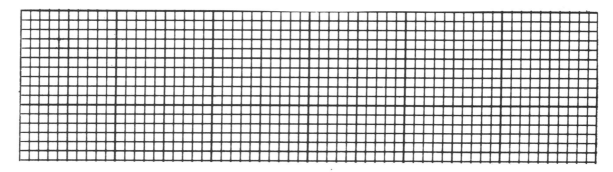

## Back stitch alphabets

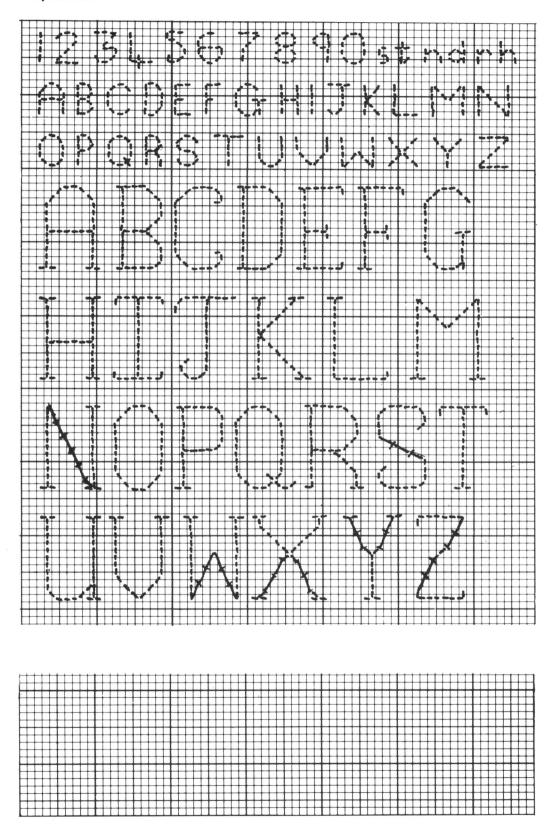

(each line on the graph represents one thread of the canvas)

# 6. Victorian pincushion 'Love'

*Materials*
canvas, 12 holes per 2.5 cm, 20 cm square
Appleton's Crewel Wool,
   2 hanks of dark pink 755
   1 hank of pink 941
gold thread, Twilley's Gold Dust (used double)
beads
   64 × 2 mm gold      136 × 2 mm green
    4 × 3 mm gold       68 × 2 mm pearl
dark pink velvet, 20 cm square
filling

**1.** Mark the centre point of the canvas, then measure 1.8 cm to the left of this spot to establish the position of the first letter. Count up three threads to reach the starting point at the top of the letter L. Thread a beading needle with white cotton, doubled, then knot the ends together. Take the needle up through the canvas at the marked point, then drop it down through the next diagonal hole and through the loop of the thread. Pull up, keeping the knot underneath the canvas, and work a small cross stitch to hold it in place.
**2.** Commence beading; bringing the needle up through the canvas, thread one pearl bead and pass the needle diagonally into the next hole above and to the right, making one tent stitch. Come out at the next hole below the first stitch and repeat the process, then continue to build up the lettering as shown on the chart, where each square represents one stitch.
**3.** Complete the central heart motif in tent stitch using pink wool, then thread the tapestry needle with gold thread and work the border around the heart. Each line represents the outer stitches forming the points, and the dot where they meet is the hole between the tent stitches of the surrounding background. The remaining space in the triangles is filled in with further straight stitches after the shapes have been established. Refer to the detailed working diagrams.
**4.** Continue to work the beaded details of hearts, leaves and flowers following the chart, and when this is complete, work the tent stitch border in gold. Fill in the entire background area with tent stitch in dark pink, and finish the embroidery with a border of satin stitch over three threads of canvas, using four strands of wool to give complete coverage.

**5.** Make up the pincushion by placing the canvas and velvet squares right sides together. Sew around the edges of the embroidery, very close to the outer row of stitches, leaving an opening on one short side. Trim the seam allowances to 1 cm. Cut the corners diagonally, close to the stitching, then turn through. Ease the corners gently into place, then stuff the pincushion very firmly with filling. Slip stitch the opening closed.

**Pattern of gold border around central heart**

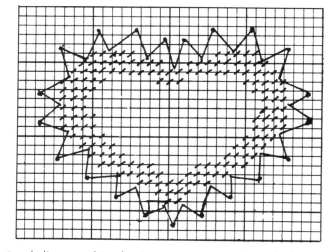

(each line on this chart represents one thread of canvas)

**Key**

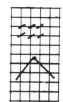

Tent stitch (pink 941)

Straight stitch (gold)

## Working chart for Victorian pincushion 'Love'

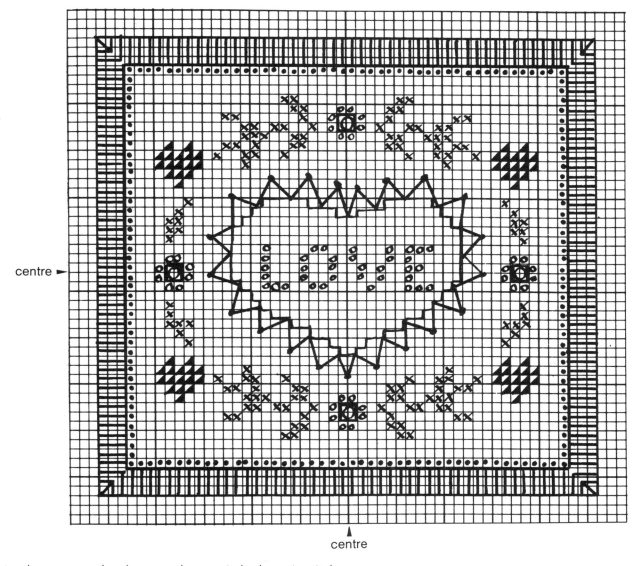

centre ▶

centre

(each square on the chart equals one stitch; the satin stitch border is worked over three threads)

**Key**

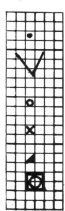

Tent stitch (gold thread)

Satin stitch (gold thread)

2 mm pearl beads

2 mm green beads

2 mm gold beads

3 mm gold beads sewn over 2 threads of canvas

# 7. Victorian pincushion 'Joy'

*Materials*
canvas, 12 holes per 2.5 cm, 18 cm square
Appleton's Crewel Wool,

| | | | |
|---|---|---|---|
| green | 256 | beige | 701 |
| red | 948 | cream | 992 |

Ribbon Floss, metallic gold
   metallic red
24 × 3 mm red beads
crimson velvet, 18 cm square
filling

**1.** Mark the centre point of the canvas and commence lettering in red metallic thread following the chart, on which each square represents one tent stitch. Next, work the central border pattern of gold and the corner leaf motifs.
**2.** Attach beads with tent stitch, using doubled sewing cotton over two threads of canvas at the points indicated on the chart.
**3.** Establish the outer edge of the pattern by sewing the gold tent stitch border, then fill in the background, using cream wool in the inner section around the lettering and beige for the remainder. Complete by working a border of satin stitch over three threads of canvas, using four strands of red wool.
**4.** Make up the pincushion by placing the velvet and canvas squares right sides together. Sew around the edges of the embroidery, very close to the outer row of stitches, leaving an opening on one short side. Trim the seam allowance to 1 cm. Cut the corners diagonally, close to the stitching, then turn through. Ease the corners gently into place, then stuff the pincushion very firmly with filling. Slip stitch the opening closed.

**Key**

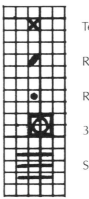

Tent stitch (green 256)

Ribbon Floss (metallic red)

Ribbon Floss (gold)

3 mm red beads

Satin stitch (red 948)

**Working chart for Victorian pincushion 'Joy'**

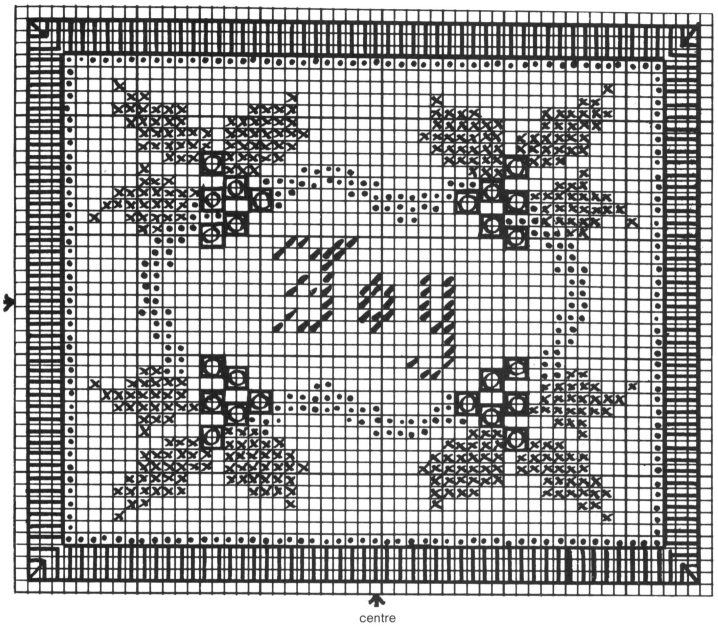

centre

(each square on the chart represents one stitch; the border
is worked over three threads of canvas)

# 8. Victorian pincushion 'Peace'

*Materials*
canvas, 12 holes per 2.5 cm, 20 cm square
Appleton's Crewel Wool, blue 745
DMC Pearl Cotton No. 5, purple 208
Ribbon Floss, silver
  iridescent pearl
Beads
  96 × 2 mm green        6 × 2 mm purple
  121 × 2 mm silver    160 × 2 mm pearl
blue velvet, 20 cm square
filling

**1.** Mark the centre of the canvas. Following the chart, on which each square represents one tent stitch, work the pattern using the threads and beads indicated.
**2.** When the tent stitch and beaded details are complete, work the tent stitch border in pearl cotton and fill in the entire background in blue crewel wool. Outline the edges of the ribbon bow with back stitch in pearl cotton, following the heavy lines on the chart.
**3.** Complete the embroidery by working a satin stitch border over three threads of canvas, using four strands of wool.
**4.** Make up the pincushion by placing the canvas and velvet squares right sides together. Sew around the edges of the embroidery, very close to the outer row of stitches, leaving an opening on one short side. Trim the seam allowance to 1 cm. Cut the corners diagonally, close to the stitching, then turn through. Ease the corners gently into place, then stuff the pincushion very firmly with filling. Slip stitch the opening closed.

**Key**

2 mm green beads

2 mm silver beads

2 mm purple beads

2 mm pearl beads

Ribbon Floss (iridescent pearl)

Ribbon Floss (silver)

DMC Pearl Cotton No. 5 (purple 208) used double for tent stitch

**Working chart for Victorian pincushion 'Peace'**

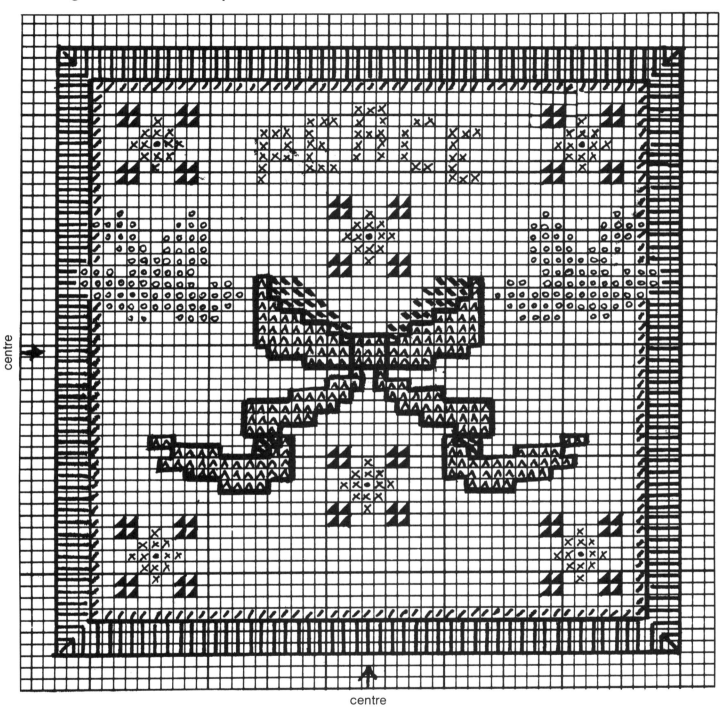

centre

centre

(each square on the graph equals one stitch; stitch the
border over three threads of canvas)

# 9. Apple blossom cushion

*Materials*
canvas, 12 holes per 2.5 cm, 50 cm square
Appleton's Crewel Wool, 1 hank each of

| | | | |
|---|---|---|---|
| dark green | 292 | dark pink | 753 |
| pale pink | 751 | yellow | 841 |

    4 hanks of light green 351
    5 hanks each of

| | | | |
|---|---|---|---|
| pale apricot | 702 | white | 991 |

pale apricot fabric, 50 cm square
cushion insert, 35 cm square

**1.** Mark the centre point of the canvas and start the stitching with a cross stitch in yellow over two threads of the canvas. Following the chart, on which each line represents one thread of the canvas, work the rest of the flower motif, then count out from the tips of the leaves to establish the position of the white frame around the motif.
**2.** After working the white stitches around the edge of the central motif, complete the design by working the surrounding four medallions, then fill in the background of each in tent stitch, using pale apricot wool.
**3.** When the five motifs are complete, work the back stitch grid pattern from the chart in white. Embroider the diamond eyelet stitches where indicated, then fill in the background area with tent stitch in light green.
**4.** Work the border of diamond eyelet stitches following the chart, then fill in the background with tent stitch in pale apricot. Stitch the outer edge of the border in back stitch over two threads of canvas using white wool.
**5.** Complete the cushion with three rows of cross stitch over two threads of the canvas, followed by two rows of tent stitch.
**6.** When the embroidery is complete, trim the edges of the canvas to approximately 2 cm in width, and place it face down over the right side of the backing fabric. Stitch around three sides of the cushion between the two outer rows of tent stitch. Trim excess fabric at the corners, then turn the cushion right side out. Insert the cushion pad, fold the raw edges to the inside and stitch the opening neatly together.

**Key**

Satin stitch (light pink 751)

Satin stitch (dark pink 753)

Cross stitch (yellow 841)

Tent stitch (light green 351)

Leaf stitch (dark green 292)

Straight stitch (white 991)

Back stitch (white 991)

Cross stitch (white 991)

Tent stitch (white 991)

Diamond eyelet (white 991)

## Working chart for apple blossom cushion

centre

centre

(each line on the graph represents one thread of canvas)

# 10. Scottie sampler

*Materials*
canvas, 12 holes per 2.5 cm, 35 × 40 cm
Appleton's Crewel Wool, 1 hank each of

| | | | |
|---|---|---|---|
| dark green | 256 | blue | 821 |
| light green | 544 | black | 993 |
| yellow | 472 | | |

2 hanks each of

| | | | |
|---|---|---|---|
| red | 447 | cream | 992 |

strong cardboard 23 × 26.5 cm

**1.** Mark the centre point of the canvas, then following the chart on page 57, on which each square represents one stitch, work the Scottie in tent stitch in black wool.
**2.** Next, work the colours of the plaid bands in alternating half cross stitch, leaving the red stitches until last. Complete the bands by filling in the areas of red, including the four corner rectangles which are worked in basketweave tent stitch.

**3.** Work the lettering around the sampler in dark green, then complete the embroidery by filling in the remaining background areas in tent stitch using cream wool.
**4.** Trim the edges of the canvas to approximately 6 cm from the stitching, and using strong thread, lace the canvas over the cardboard panel firmly and evenly, ready for framing.

**Key**

Blue 821

Dark green 256

Black 993

Yellow 472

Light green 544

Cream 992

Project 12: Dovecote wedding sampler

Project 13: Photo frame mat

## Working chart for Scottie sampler

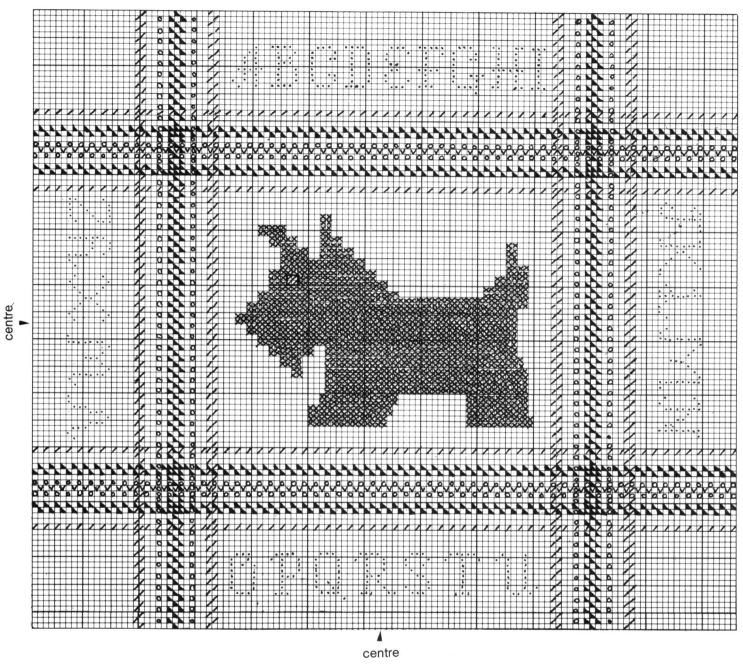

centre

centre

(each square on the chart represents one stitch)

# 11. Teddy bear birth sampler

## Materials

canvas, 12 holes per 2.5 cm, 35 × 40 cm
Appleton's Crewel Wool, 1 hank each of

| | | | |
|---|---|---|---|
| tan | 695 | white | 991 |
| dark pink | 944 | cream | 992 |
| light pink | 752 | black | 993 |
| dark blue | 742 | brown | 303 |
| light blue | 461 | beige-gold | 692 |

2 hanks each of

| | | | |
|---|---|---|---|
| apricot | 702 | peach | 701 |

strong cardboard 22.5 × 28.5 cm

**1.** Mark the centre point of the canvas. Count down 6 threads, then begin working two threads to the left of this point, at the base of the bear's tummy panel. Follow Chart A, on which each square represents one stitch, and work the bear in tent stitch, leaving the heart, nose and facial features until last.

**2.** When the bear is complete, add the heart and nose details in satin stitch, then backstitch the mouth in black on top of the beige muzzle area.

**3.** Using the alphabet chart with extra graph lines (see page 44), draw out the lettering required. Count the total width of stitches needed and divide in half to calculate the centre point. Matching this centre line with the centre line of the sampler chart, embroider the lettering in place using brown wool. If the chosen name is longer than the space allowed in the pattern, move the side curves outwards by an even number of spaces at either end to allow for it. When the lettering is complete, work the background oval in tent stitch, using cream wool. Note that for clarity only the stitches around the edge of the oval are shown on the chart. Work these first, then fill in the remaining area around the lettering. Finish by stitching the vertical lines of tent stitch in the background with light blue.

**4.** Next, work from Chart B, on which each line represents one thread of the canvas. Start by filling in the stripes in the background of the bear, alternating brick stitch in apricot using four strands of wool and mosaic stitch in peach using three strands, placed as shown on the chart.

**5.** Stitch the border as shown on the chart, using four strands of dark blue for the satin stitch and three strands for the rest of the stitches. Complete the sampler with three rows of tent stitch in dark blue.

**6.** Trim the edges of the canvas to approximately 6 cm from the stitching, and use a long length of strong thread to lace it firmly over the card ready for framing.

## Key

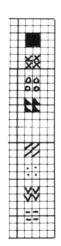

Black 993

White 991

Light pink 752

Dark blue 742

Light blue 461
Beige-gold 692

Cream 992

Tan 695

# Working charts for teddy bear birth sampler

Chart A

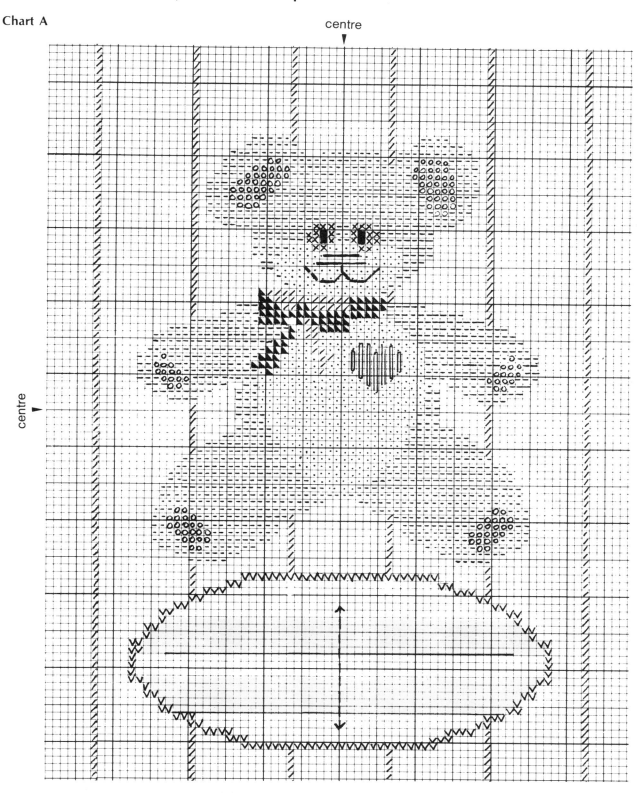

(each square on the chart represents one stitch)

**Chart B**

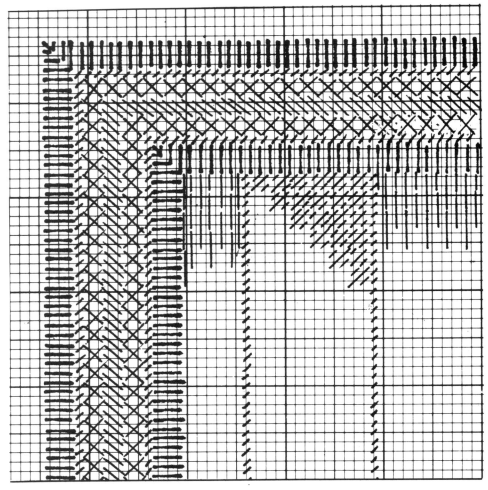

(each line on the chart represents one thread of canvas)

**Key**

*Background*

Tent stitch (blue 461)

Brick stitch (apricot 702)

Mosaic stitch (peach 701)

*Border*

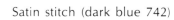

Satin stitch (dark blue 742)

Tent stitch (white 991)

Cross stitch (light pink 752)

Slanted Gobelin stitch (white 991)

60

# 12. Dovecote wedding sampler

*Materials*
brown perforated paper, 1 sheet 35 × 22.5 cm
DMC Stranded Cotton, 1 skein each of

| | | | | |
|---|---|---|---|---|
| white | | dark blue | 813 |
| ecru | | cream | 739 |
| brown | 898 | yellow | 725 |
| dark brown | 3371 | grey | 762 |
| light apricot | 819 | light green | 523 |
| dark apricot | 353 | dark green | 522 |
| light blue | 800 | | |

**1.** Following the graph, on which the lines represent the grid of the paper, start the embroidery at the bottom left hand corner, 2 cm in from each edge. Work the scalloped border in cross stitch, using three strands of ecru cotton.

**2.** Next, work the blue flowers using 6 strands of cotton for the petals and 3 for the yellow cross stitches at the centres. Finish the border with triple oblong cross stitches in light green between the flowers, using 6 strands.

**3.** Following the chart and counting out from the border, work the doves in cross stitch, using 3 strands, with highlights in grey. Work the flower wreaths in the colours indicated using 6 strands throughout, and the white hearts in cross stitch using 3 strands. The date banner is outlined in back stitch using 3 strands of ecru cotton, and the dovecote is embroidered with 6 strands for all stitches.

**4.** From the back stitch alphabet charts (page 45) choose the initials to go inside the flower wreaths. Use a pencil to fill them in on the sampler chart before embroidering them in back stitch using 3 strands of brown cotton.

**5.** Using the smaller letters on the chart, graph the date required for the banner onto the section of blank graph paper. Count the number of stitches used for the completed date, and divide this figure in half to determine the centre point. Match the centre line of the date graph with the centre line on the banner and embroider the details required.

**6.** Trim the perforated paper to 1 cm from the outside stitches of the border pattern before framing.

**Key**

## Working chart for dovecote sampler

centre ▶

▲ centre

(each line on the chart represents one grid of the paper)

# Mounting an embroidered panel

Measure the finished embroidery and cut a piece of thick cardboard to the exact size. Use a craft knife with a metal-edged rule to do this as accurately as possible, making sure that the corners are square.

Cut the excess canvas from the embroidery, leaving a margin of 3.5 cm for turnings.

If the work appears to be distorted, block it back into shape—using a firm surface larger than the embroidery but soft enough to take pins, e.g. a cork board or insulation fibreboard, draw two lines at right angles to each other, crossing at a point about 7.5 cm from one corner. Pin a corner of the finished embroidery face down to this exact spot, then flatten it out and pin one edge along the marked line at intervals of 2 cm. Pin the second side in the same manner to the other line. Mist the back of the work with water from a fine nozzled spray bottle, just enough to make it damp without saturating it. You will then find that you are able to pull the canvas back into shape. Use a ruler and set square to align the free corner and pin it into position. Pin the remaining two sides to the board and leave the piece for a day or two to dry out. When the pins are removed, it should be the correct shape; if it is not, repeat the procedure.

When the canvas has been trimmed and straightened, place it face down on a table and position the cardboard panel over the embroidery. Turn the corners of the canvas over the card and then fold the sides over, forming mitred corners. Pin along the top edge of the embroidery, through the edge of the cardboard. Repeat this procedure at the bottom edge, pulling the canvas firmly between them. Do the same with the two side edges.

Use a long length of strong linen upholstery thread in a large-eyed needle to lace the canvas tightly across the back of the card from one side to the other. Repeat this procedure with the other two sides. Sew the edges of the corners together. Check on the front of the work that the rows of stitches lie parallel to the edges of the card, and make any adjustments necessary at this stage before framing the piece.

Needlepoint in woollen yarns should not be framed under glass. Wool needs to breathe, and in some climatic conditions moisture from the fibres can condense on the glass and cause problems. Needlepoint in wool is very durable, and will respond well to being vacuumed with a soft dusting brush every few weeks. Some embroiderers use upholstery fabric protectors on their finished pieces, but it is wise to test them out on a sample beforehand as some chemicals used in wool dyes might react with them.

Needlepoint with stranded cotton, pearl cotton, metallic threads or ribbon presents no problem when framed under glass. The non-reflective type of glass will protect it well and allow it to be seen to best advantage, so it is worth paying a little extra for this type of glass. It is also possible to purchase glass which will protect your work from ultraviolet rays; although more expensive, this may be the best type to use on a piece which will be displayed in a fairly sunny position.

Finally, a word of warning: take care choosing your framer. Mount your work yourself unless you are sure that he or she knows how to do it properly. It will take you many hours to stitch a project and an inept framer can ruin it in minutes, and charge you a fortune for doing so.

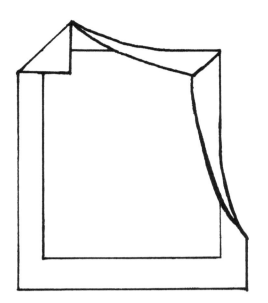

Turn the corners of the fabric over the card. Turn the sides of the fabric over the card.

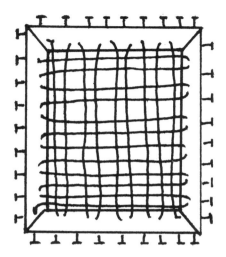

Pin the fabric to the card around all sides. Lace the embroidery to the card from top to bottom, then from side to side, using strong linen thread.

# 13. Photo frame mat

*Materials*
white perforated paper, 1 sheet 35 × 22.5 cm
DMC Stranded Cotton, 1 skein each of

| | | | |
|---|---|---|---|
| white | | light pink | 819 |
| green | 369 | dark pink | 963 |
| yellow | 744 | | |

pink mat board 26 × 21 cm

**1.** Following the chart, on which the lines represent the grid of the paper, begin the design at the bottom left hand corner, 2 cm in from each edge. Work the outer border in cross stitch, using three strands of white cotton.

**2.** Work the four corner motifs in white cross stitch as shown, and link them with the two inner border rows of cross stitch.

**3.** Use the full six strands of cotton to work the remaining embroidery. With yellow, work the flower centres in satin stitch as shown, then embroider the flowers in satin stitch, using light pink for the petals and dark pink for their edges. Work the corner hearts in dark pink, then complete the motifs with four Roumanian stitch leaves as shown on the chart, and work stems of horizontal Van Dyke stitch next to them.

**4.** Complete the embroidery by working the background grid pattern in back stitch using white cotton.

**5.** Using a sharp craft knife, carefully cut away the central rectangle of the paper along the next row of holes beyond the inner row of stitches. Trim the outer edge of the design 2 mm outside the stitches using sharp pointed scissors.

**6.** Mount the photograph using double-sided tape in each corner, taking care to place it centrally on the rectangle of pink mat board. Apply small pieces of tape to the back of the embroidery behind the corner hearts and central flowers, then carefully position the needlepoint over the photograph and press firmly in place. The assembled piece can then be framed.

**Key**

Satin stitch (dark pink 963)

Satin stitch (light pink 819)

Satin stitch (yellow 744)

Roumanian leaf (green 369)

Back stitch (white)

Cross stitch (white)

Horizontal Van Dyke (green 369)

# Working chart for photo frame mat

centre

centre

(each line on the chart represents one grid of the paper)

# 14. Jewel case

*Materials*

plastic canvas, 1 sheet 35 × 27 cm, 10 holes per 2.5 cm
Appleton's Crewel Wools, 5 skeins blue 461
   1 skein each of
   cream        992         pale green     351
   mid green   353
gold Ribbon Floss
DMC Pearl Cotton No. 3, pink 818
silk ribbons, 3 mm wide,
   light apricot             dark apricot
   mid apricot             light pink
30 cm lining fabric, 115 cm wide
45 cm zip fastener, sky blue
press stud, 10 mm diameter
Fusible Fleece, 25.5 × 19 cm
3 × 8 cm squares wadding
heavyweight interfacing, 16 × 1.8 cm
perforated paper, 9.5 × 2.5 cm
40 cm lace, 15 mm wide with slots for ribbon along one
   edge
7.5 cm elastic, 10 mm wide
thin white card, 1 piece 19 × 25.5 cm
   2 pieces 41 × 1 cm

**1.** Count 12 threads from the top and side edges at one corner of the sheet of plastic canvas to establish the starting point for the embroidery. Thread the needle with 55 cm of gold ribbon floss and use a small piece of sticky tape to secure the end to the back of the canvas, close to the edge.
**2.** Following Chart A, on which each line represents one thread of the canvas, come up at point A and lay the ribbon floss strand flat along the canvas, going through to the back again at point B on the chart. Come up at point C and take a long stitch, keeping the ribbon floss flat again, and going down at point D. Repeat the process through the points marked E, F and G, and finish by taking the thread to the back of the canvas at point H and securing the end with another piece of sticky tape. (The pieces of tape will be removed when the ends of the ribbon floss have been 'buried' in the subsequent embroidery.)
**3.** Using a second length of ribbon floss, repeat Step 2 following the small letters a to h on the chart.
**4.** Thread the needle with pearl cotton in pink and work tent stitch in groups of three stitches as indicated on the chart, couching down the ribbon floss, and leaving one thread of plastic canvas showing in between the gold

borders. Work tent stitch in cream wool over this thread, leaving 1 thread unworked in each corner.
**5.** Change to Chart B to work the remaining embroidery. The previously worked gold and cream borders are shown as a shaded area on this chart, edged with the tent stitches worked in pink pearl cotton.
**6.** Use dark apricot ribbon to work the centres of the corner flowers in Smyrna cross stitch, and complete them with straight stitches using pale apricot ribbon, following the detailed diagram. Try to keep the ribbon flat and untwisted while forming the stitches. Add the green leaves using crewel wool in lazy daisy stitch loops following the chart.
**7.** Work the chequer stitch border around the edge of the embroidery using 3 strands of blue crewel wool.
**8.** Following the chart, work the flower wreath using ribbon colours and stitches as indicated. Work the desired initial in gold ribbon floss, following the alphabet chart on page 72, and centering the letter within the central shaded area of Chart B.
**9.** Complete the front of the jewel case by working the entire background area inside the couched borders and flower wreath in basketweave tent stitch using 3 strands of cream wool.
**10.** Refer to Chart C, on which each square represents 3 meshes of the canvas, and work the following blocks of chequer stitch in blue crewel wool to complete the back, spine and side edges of the jewellery case.
1. Spine   3 × 25 blocks of stitches
2. Back   15 × 25 blocks of stitches
3. and 4. Long side edges   1 × 25 blocks of stitches each
5–8. Short side edges   1 × 14 blocks of stitches each
**11.** Cut out all pieces of embroidery leaving one thread beyond the stitching all round. Place the spine section on the left hand side of the front panel, wrong sides together, and oversew the two pieces together with 3 strands of blue wool, lining up the holes and making a stitch in each one, over the bare threads at the edges. In the same way, join the back panel to the opposite side of the spine.
**12.** Join a short strip to each end of the two long pieces for the side edges, then line the joins up with the corners of the back and front panels along the opening edges of the case. Oversew the strips to the back and front panels, noting that the shorter strips do not quite reach the spine.
**13.** Oversew all the remaining bare edges around the case: across the spine between the two side sections and around the ends of the side pieces.

**14.** Insert the zip. Fold the excess tape at the top of the zip back to the wrong side beyond the metal stops at the top of the zip. Open the fastener, and pin the tapes in place on the inside of the sides of the jewel case, starting at the top. The teeth of the zipper should just protrude beyond the side pieces of the case. When the zip is fully pinned in place, tuck the remaining part inside the spine and pin securely. Test that the slide can run freely, and ensure that the corners of the two sides of the case are meeting correctly. Back stitch the zip in place with matching sewing cotton used double.

**15.** From lining fabric cut the following pieces:
2 strips 43 × 4 cm for sides
1 piece 30 × 24 cm for main panel
1 piece each
    12 × 5.5 cm for ring roll
    12 × 1.7 cm for top of earring panel
    12 cm square for brooch pad
    18.5 × 5.5 cm for chain holder
    12 × 4.5 cm for elasticated strip

**16.** Round the corners of the piece of Fusible Fleece, then centre the main fabric panel on top of it, right side up, and bond the two together following the manufacturer's instructions. Set aside while preparing the remaining pieces.

**17.** *Ring roll* Fold the fabric strip in half, right sides together, and seam across one short end and down the long side. Turn through to the right side and stuff the tube with scraps of wadding. Turn in the raw edges at the open end and slip stitch them together.

*Earring holder* Round two corners on one long side of the perforated paper strip and use the fabric strip to bind the straight top edge.

*Brooch pillow* Stack 3 square pieces of wadding on top of each other and centre them on the wrong side of the fabric square. Turn all raw edges over the wadding and pin and tack the turnings in place.

*Chain holder* Turn the raw edges to the wrong side and wrap the fabric around the strip of heavyweight interfacing. Slip stitch the ends and edges together neatly to completely enclose the stiffening.

*Elasticated strip* Fold the fabric strip in half lengthwise, wrong sides together, and seam the long sides. Turn the tube through to the right side and thread the elastic through it. Turn in the raw edges at each end and stitch securely through both the fabric and elastic to hold it in place.

**18.** Following the layout diagram on page 72, sew the accessories in place on top of the fleece-backed panel of fabric. Sew half of the press stud to the underside of the end of the ring roll, and the other section in a corresponding position on the base fabric. Thread narrow ribbon through the insertion slots in the lace edging and hand sew it around the edge of the brooch cushion, covering the top stitching. Start at the centre top of the square and mitre the corners of the lace. Cover the join with a bow of ribbon.

**19.** Round the corners of the largest piece of card and score two lines across it as shown in the diagram on page 72. Mount the finished lining panel over this card with the ring roll, earring holder and brooch panel over the narrower

section A. Glue all turnings down smoothly to the wrong side of the card.

**20.** Fold the two long pieces of fabric lengthwise and press. Slip a long strip of card inside each one and push it up against the fold. Turn in and glue the raw edges at each end. Glue the long strips around each side of the case on the inside, over the zipper tapes, with the surplus material lying flat against the base panels of the case. Test to ensure that the zip will work freely and adjust the strips if necessary.

**21.** Glue the covered card securely into position covering the raw edges of fabric on the side strips.

## Working charts for jewel case

**Chart A**

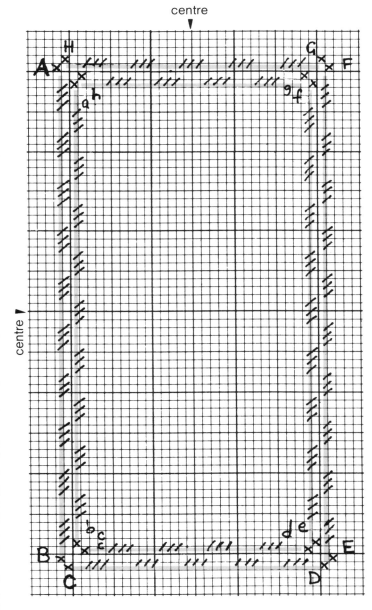

(each line of the graph represents one thread of canvas)

**Chart B**

centre

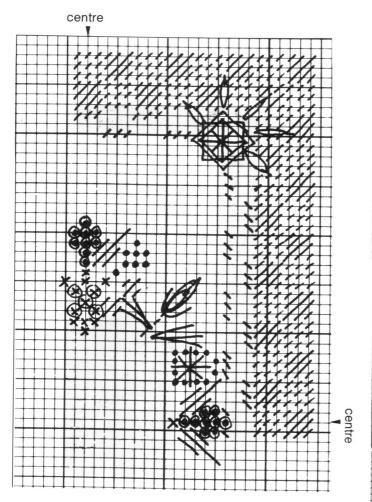

(each line on the graph represents one thread of canvas)

| | |
|---|---|
| French knot (dark apricot ribbon) | |
| French knot (pink Pearl Cotton) | |
| Smyrna cross stitch (light apricot ribbon) | |
| Double lazy daisy loops (mid apricot ribbon) | |
| Mosaic stitch (light green wool 351) | |
| Straight stitch (light green wool 351) | |
| Cross stitch (light green wool 351) | |
| Smyrna cross stitch (dark apricot ribbon) | |
| Cross stitch (light apricot ribbon) | |
| Cross stitch (mid green wool 353) | |
| Fly stitch (mid green wool 353) | |
| Back stitch (mid green wool 353) | |
| Straight stitch (mid green wool 353) | |
| Lazy daisy stitch (mid green wool 353) | |
| Straight stitch (light apricot ribbon) | |

**Detail diagram of corner flower**

Key

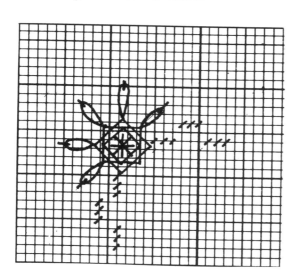

(each line on the graph represents one thread of canvas)

Smyrna cross stitch (dark apricot ribbon)

Straight stitches (pale apricot ribbon)

Lazy daisy loops (mid green wool 353)

Tent stitch (pink Pearl Cotton)

**Chart C**

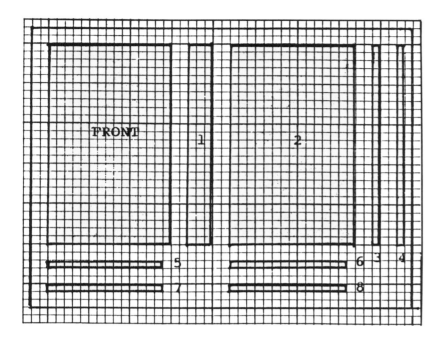

(each square on the graph equals one block of chequer stitch over three threads of the canvas)

**Key**
1. Spine
2. Back
3 and 4. Long side edges
5–8. Short side edges

**Alphabet chart for jewel case initials**

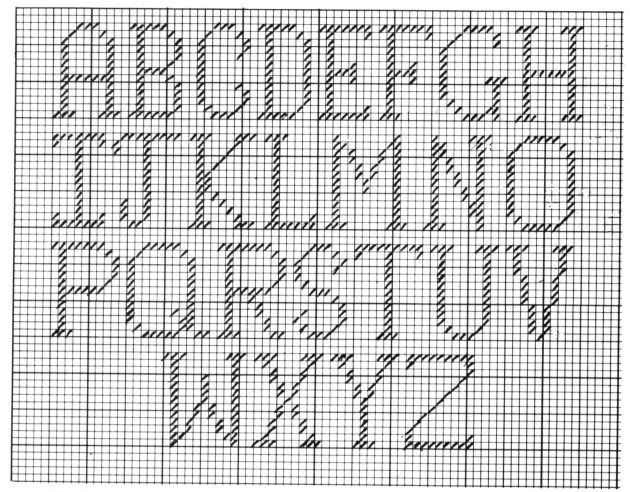

(one square of the chart represents one stitch)

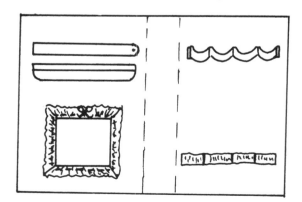

Jewel case lining—layout diagram

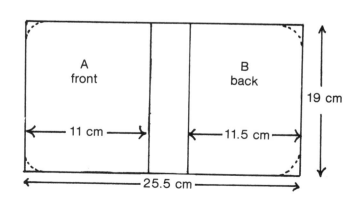

Lining card—cutting diagram

Project 14: Jewel case exterior

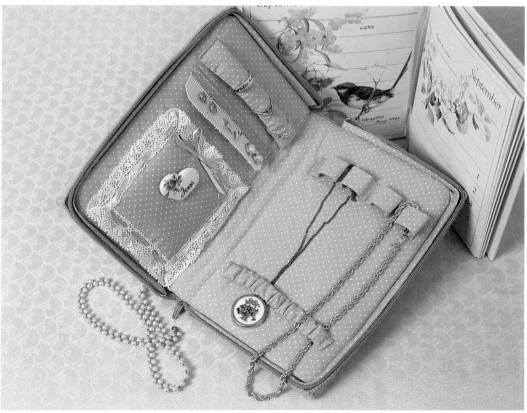

Project 14: Jewel case interior

Project 16: Petit point button brooch

Projects 15 and 17: Fob brooch and petit point pendant

# 15. Fob brooch

*Materials*
gold bow brooch pin
oval pendant frame 2 × 2.5 cm
5 cm square silk gauze with 30 threads per 2.5 cm
3 cm square thin white card
DMC Stranded Cotton,

| | | | |
|---|---|---|---|
| brown | 437 | green | 772 |
| dark pink | 604 | light pink | 818 |
| yellow | 744 | | |

**1.** Use one strand of cotton for all stitching. Take care not to carry any threads across the background; because it is left unworked, any untidy ends will show on the completed embroidery. Start with the yellow cross stitch at the centre of the flower, placing it 2 cm from the top and left hand side edges of the piece of silk gauze.

**2.** Following the chart, on which each line represents one thread of the canvas, work the light and dark petals and the leaves in satin stitch, and the stem of the flower in back stitch.

**3.** Work the flowerpot in satin stitch using brown thread.

**4.** Cut an oval of white card to fit inside the aperture of the pendant frame. Centre the stitched flower over this and trim the edges of the gauze to 3 mm beyond the edge of the card. Run a line of glue around the edge of the card at the back and fold the turnings evenly over it, pressing the gauze down firmly all round.

**5.** Coat the inside of the frame with glue and allow it to become slightly tacky. Press the embroidered oval firmly into the frame and hold it down for a few minutes until the glue has set. Mount the frame onto the bow pin using the jump ring provided.

## Working chart for fob brooch

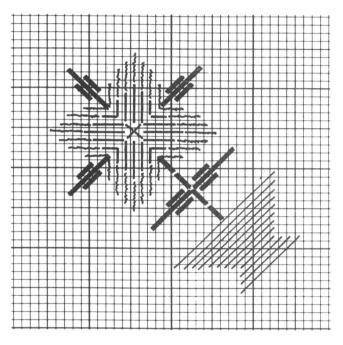

(each line of the graph represents one thread of the canvas)

### Key

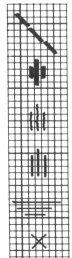

Back stitch over 2 threads (green 772)

Straight stitch (green 772)

Satin stitch (dark pink 604)

Satin stitch (light pink 818)

Satin stitch (brown 437)

Cross stitch over 2 threads (yellow 744)

# 16. Petit point button brooch

## Materials

Lugano fabric, 6 cm square, 26 threads per 2.5 cm
DMC Stranded Cotton,

| | | | |
|---|---|---|---|
| purple | 208 | gold | 725 |
| dark pink | 223 | blue | 794 |
| light green | 320 | light pink | 819 |
| dark green | 520 | mid pink | 3689 |

brooch pin, 2.5 cm
covered button kit components, 27 mm diameter
small scrap white card
15 cm lace edging, 15 mm wide
15 cm thin gold tinsel cord

**1.** Embroider the motif from the chart, on which each square represents one stitch, using tent stitch over one thread of the fabric. Work with one strand of cotton doubled.
**2.** When the embroidery is complete, lightly press it on the wrong side then cut it into a circle 4.5 cm in diameter, with the embroidery in the centre.
**3.** Cover the button shape with the circle of fabric following the manufacturer's instructions.
**4.** Using a sharp craft knife, carefully cut the shank off the button level with the back. File off any remaining nub so that the back is perfectly flat.
**5.** Gather the lace edging to fit around the edge of the button and glue in place.
**6.** Glue the gold cord around the edge of the button above the lace, with the ends meeting smoothly at the bottom of the design.
**7.** Cut a cardboard circle to fit the back of the button and glue in place. You may wish to cover this first in either decorative paper or thin fabric.
**8.** Glue the brooch pin to the centre of the card circle, making sure that the design is properly aligned and will sit straight when worn.

## Working chart for petit point button brooch

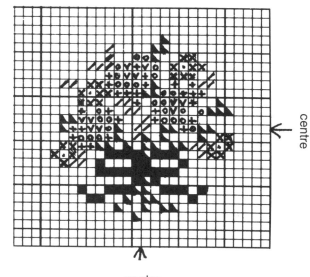

centre

centre

(each square on the chart represents one tent stitch)

### Key

| | |
|---|---|
| ■ | Purple 208 |
| X | Blue 794 |
| ⋮ | Gold 725 |
| ◥ | Dark green 520 |
| ⁄ | Light green 320 |
| V | Dark pink 223 |
| o o | Mid pink 3689 |
| ⊞ | Light pink 819 |

# 17. Petit point pendant

*Materials*
pendant frame, 25 mm diameter
silk gauze, 5 cm square, 30 holes per 2.5 cm
Rajmahal Art Silks,

| | | | |
|---|---|---|---|
| laurel green | 65 | Boston tan | 173 |
| chardonnay | 93 | gentle | |
| imperial | | magenta | 181 |
| purple | 115 | vibrant musk | 184 |
| bluebell | 121 | maidenhair | 521 |
| woodlands | 171 | | |

**1.** Using 1 strand of thread doubled for all stitching, work the motif in tent stitch on the centre of the piece of gauze, following the chart, on which each square represents one stitch. Take care not to leave any threads loose at the back of the work; because the background is left unstitched, any loose ends or threads 'jumped' from one area to another will be visible.

**2.** Separate the components of the pendant frame and centre the embroidery over the white card disc. Trim the gauze to 3 mm outside the edge of the card and apply glue to the edges on the wrong side. Turn the 3 mm allowance over the card, pressing it into the glue as smoothly as possible. Leave to dry.

**3.** Re-assemble the frame, placing the embroidery between the clear disc at the front and the backing card. Make sure that the motif is sitting straight in the frame, then bend in the fasteners at the back to hold the contents in place. Mount the pendant on a matching chain.

*Note* The working chart lists the colours and numbers for Rajmahal Silks, followed by the equivalent shades of DMC Stranded Cotton. Cotton does not have the beautiful sheen of the silk but is easier to work with and less expensive.

## Working chart for petit point pendant

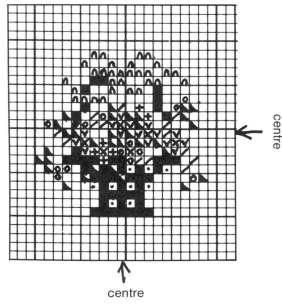

centre

centre

(each square on the graph represents one tent stitch)

**Key**

| | Rajmahal Silks | DMC Stranded Cotton |
|---|---|---|
| | Laurel green 65 | 890 |
| | Chardonnay 93 | 725 |
| | Imperial purple 115 | 550 |
| | Bluebell 121 | 793 |
| | Woodlands 171 | 437 |
| | Boston tan 173 | 632 |
| | Gentle magenta 181 | 3608 |
| | Vibrant musk 184 | 718 |
| | Maidenhair 521 | 581 |

# 18. Button earrings

## Materials

*Materials*
2 × 22 mm 'Creative Buttons'
DMC Stranded Cotton,
   ecru
   dark peach   760
DMC Pearl Cotton No. 3,
   light green   472         peach    754
   dark green   581
1 pair of earring backs

**1.** Using a sharp craft knife, cut the shanks off the buttons as close to the surface as possible.
**2.** Using the full 6 strands of ecru stranded cotton, work 4 buttonhole stitches into each of the holes around the edge of the button shape.
**3.** Take a doubled strand of ecru stranded cotton and work one Smyrna cross stitch across the centre of the shape, using the ring of 8 inner holes. Repeat this a second time on top of the first stitch and fasten off the threads securely.
**4.** With light green pearl cotton, oversew the remaining bar of the button; 2 stitches in each space should cover it well.
**5.** Work back stitch through the remaining spaces between the light green bar and the outer edge of ecru buttonhole stitch using dark green pearl cotton doubled.
**6.** Using 6 threads of dark peach stranded cotton for the centre, and a single thickness of apricot pearl cotton for the outer petals, work a bullion stitch rose across the centre of the shape, covering the ecru Smyrna cross stitch foundation.
**7.** Repeat these steps to make the second earring, then glue the earring backs to the centre back of each one.

## Working chart for button earrings

*Edge:* Buttonhole stitch over Bar 3
*Between bars 2 and 3:* Back stitch
*Centre:* Smyrna cross stitch
*Bar 2:* Oversewn

## Bullion stitch roses

A single bullion stitch is worked as shown in the diagram. Bring the thread out at point B, then take the needle to point A and insert it through the backing, coming out again at point B. Wrap the thread firmly but not tightly over the point of the needle several times, until the wraps equal the length of the space between A and B. Holding the wrapped thread down firmly with your thumb, pull the needle through the loops and gently stroke the wrapped thread into place.

The rose is constructed of a number of bullion stitches. Start in the centre with two in the darker colour lying next to each other, then surround these with a spiral formation of about 5 more stitches in a lighter tone.

Working bullion stitch

A bullion stitch rose

# 19. Red and gold drop earrings

*Materials*
plastic canvas, 10 holes per 2.5 cm, 5.5 cm square
DMC Stranded Cotton, scarlet 817
gold Ribbon Floss
1 pair gold French ear wires
4 × 2 mm gold beads
4 × 3 mm red beads
2 × 6 mm gold bugle beads
beading thread

**1.** Following the cutting chart, carefully cut 2 shapes from the piece of plastic canvas.
**2.** Following the stitching chart, use gold ribbon floss to work a diamond eyelet stitch over three threads into the central hole. Using 6 strands of red stranded cotton, work cross stitches around the eyelet stitch.
**3.** Finish the edge of the shape by oversewing it with gold ribbon floss.
**4.** Using beading thread doubled, attached securely to the top hole of the plastic canvas shape, thread on one gold bead, one red, one bugle bead, another red bead and a final gold one. Pass the thread through the hole at the base of the ear wire, then back through the five beads from top to bottom. Secure the thread as invisibly as possible into the embroidery and snip off excess. A dab of clear glue will help to hold it securely.
**5.** Repeat steps 1 to 4 to make the second earring.

**Key**

Diamond eyelet (gold ribbon floss)

Cross stitch (scarlet stranded cotton)

Oversewing the edge (gold ribbon floss)

**Cutting chart**

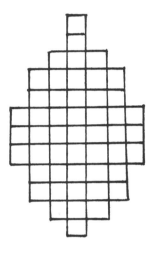

**Stitching chart**

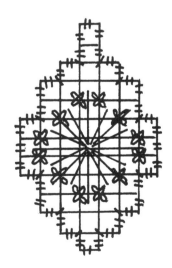

# 20. Satin stitch bookmark

## Materials

25 cm blue grosgrain ribbon, 24 mm wide
canvas, 18 holes per 2.5 cm, 9 × 28 cm strip
DMC Stranded Cotton,

| | | | |
|---|---|---|---|
| dark green | 502 | pink | 3689 |
| light green | 503 | light blue | 3756 |
| blue | 799 | | |

**1.** Following Chart A, on which each thread of the canvas is represented by one line of the graph, work the block pattern 5 times, starting 5 cm from one short end of the canvas. Use the full 6 strands of cotton throughout.

**2.** Work the block pattern from Chart B for the centre section.

**3.** Turn Chart A upsidedown and work 4 more complete blocks before finishing the bookmark with the partial block shown on Chart C, which forms the bottom point.

**4.** Trim the canvas on the short top edge and the two long sides to 6 threads outside the embroidery. Press the turnings to the back. Trim the edges of the pointed end to a similar width and fold these turnings to the back of the bookmark as smoothly as possible with no canvas showing at the edges.

**5.** Slip stitch the ribbon along the back of the bookmark as invisibly as possible, turning under 5 mm on the top edge. Trim the bottom end to the shape of the point on the canvas, allowing 5 mm for turning to the inside. Fold this seam allowance underneath the ribbon and finish slip stitching it in place to line the bookmark.

**6.** Make a 5 cm long tassel from blue stranded cotton and sew it to the point of the bookmark.

**Key**

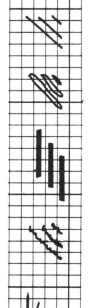

Dark green 502

Light green 503

Dark blue 799

Light blue 3756

Pink 3689 (diamond eyelet stitch)

## Working charts for satin stitch bookmark

### Chart A

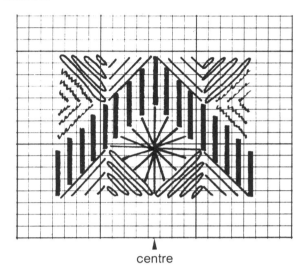

centre

### Chart B

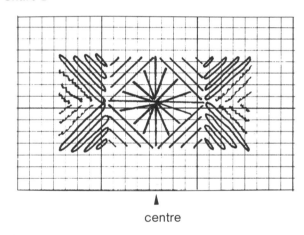

centre

### Chart C

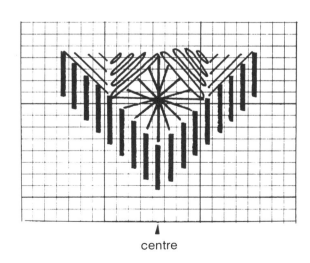

centre

(each line of the graph represents one thread of canvas)

## Making a tassel

Cut a piece of medium-weight card 1 cm longer than the desired length of the finished tassel and approximately twice as wide. Wrap the thread over the card about 30 times, then thread a needle with 30 cm of yarn and pass it through the loops along the top edge. Tie the ends of the yarn in a tight knot, gathering all the loops of thread, and clip the ends 5 cm from the knot.

Cut the opposite ends of the thread loops and remove the card. Pass the threaded needle through the bunch of strands, 2 cm below the knot and wind the thread around them a couple of times. Sew through from side to side to anchor the binding thread in place, and finish off by threading the end downwards through the centre of the strands. Trim the bottom ends of the tassel by approximately 1 cm so that they are level, and use the 5 cm tails from the top knot to sew the tassel in place on the embroidery.

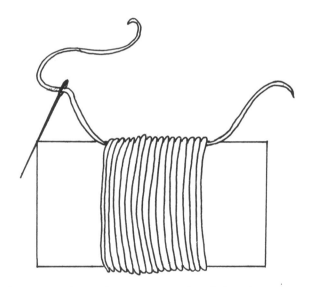

*Making a tassel:* Wind yarn over card and thread tying strand through top loops.

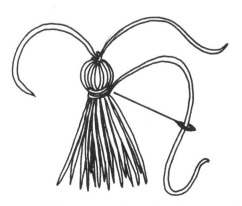

*Finishing a tassel:* Cut bottom loops, bind together 2 cm from top knot, and use tie ends to secure tassel to embroidery.

# 21. Beaded bookmark

## Materials

canvas, 14 holes per 2.5 cm, 7.5 × 14 cm
gold Ribbon Floss
Appleton's Crewel Wool, cream 991
DMC Pearl Cotton No. 3,

| | | | |
|---|---|---|---|
| light green | 472 | yellow | 745 |
| dark green | 581 | pink | 818 |

64 × 2 mm iridescent blue beads
50 cm blue grosgrain ribbon 24 mm wide
2 × 4 cm squares of blue felt

**1.** Mark the starting point 3.5 cm from the top edge of the canvas midway between each long side and start stitching following the chart, on which each line represents one thread of the canvas. Use yellow pearl cotton to work the Smyrna cross stitch in the centre of the design.

**2.** Work the beading using cream sewing cotton in the same way as for the Victorian pincushion designs, and finish off the ends securely.

**3.** Work the remaining stitches in pearl cotton from the centre of the motif outwards using the colours as shown on the chart, then embroider the gold cross stitch border in ribbon floss.

**4.** Complete the motif with the blocks of white satin stitch using 3 strands of crewel wool.

**5.** Turn the canvas round and work a second motif in the remaining space following the previous steps.

**6.** Trim the canvas squares to 4 threads from the edge of the stitching all round, then fold the turnings to the back of the embroidery so that no blank canvas shows around the edges.

**7.** Fold the ends of the ribbon to the wrong side, forming a point at each end, and slip stitch them in place with matching sewing cotton so that no raw edges are left exposed. Pin the canvas squares to the ribbon with one corner positioned 6.5 cm from each point. Cover the back of the shape, including the ribbon, with a square of matching felt, and slip stitch the felt to the canvas all round each motif. Tie a very loose overhand knot in the centre of the ribbon.

## Working chart for beaded bookmark

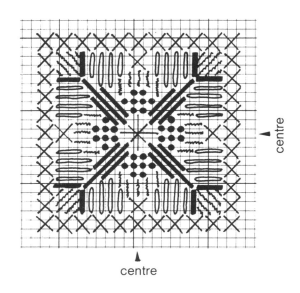

(each line of the graph represents one thread of canvas)

## Key

Double cross stitch (yellow pearl cotton)

Beaded tent stitch (blue beads)

Cross stitch over 2 threads (gold ribbon floss)

Straight stitch (light green pearl cotton)

Straight stitch (dark green pearl cotton)

Satin stitch (pink pearl cotton)

Satin stitch (white pearl cotton)

Projects 15, 16, 17, 18 and 19: Brooches, pendants and earrings

Projects 20, 21 and 22: Satin stitch, beaded and perforated bookmarks

Project 23: Photo album cover

Project 24: Blue spectacles case

Project 25: Beige spectacles case

# 22. Perforated paper bookmark

## Working chart for perforated paper bookmark

*Materials*
1 black bookmark card mount
perforated paper, white, 17 × 6 cm
DMC Stranded Cotton,
    dark pink      223          light pink        776
    dark green   520

**1.** Mark a point 2 cm in from the top and side edges of the perforated paper, and start stitching with the full 6 strands of cotton in dark green. Work the cross stitch border following the chart, on which each line represents one grid line of the perforated paper.
**2.** After completing the border, work the horizontal bars as shown on the chart in rows of trammed Gobelin stitch in pink, bordered with rows of cross stitch in green.
**3.** Fill each space with the flower motif as shown, then trim the edges of the bookmark to 1 cm outside the stitching. Position it inside the card mount and mark any white areas showing outside the border cross stitching. Use dark green cotton to fill them in with tent stitch.
**4.** Glue the completed bookmark behind the opening of the mounting card, then fold the flap of the card into place over the back of the perforated paper and glue it down around the edges. The remaining fold of the card can be left free to write a message, or it can be glued in place behind the first fold.

## Key

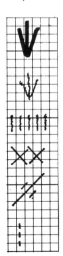

Straight stitch (dark pink 223)

Straight stitch (light pink 776)

Gobelin stitch (light pink 776)

Cross stitch (green 520)

Straight stitch (green 520)

Back stitch (green 520)

(each line of the graph represents one grid of the paper)

# 23. Photo album cover

## Materials

Penelope double-thread canvas, 10 holes per 2.5 cm, 35 cm
   square
photo album 25.5 × 29.5 cm
0.5 m dusty pink upholstery fabric 120 cm wide
wadding 50 × 30 cm
2 pieces thin white card 22.5 × 28.5 cm
1 m thick cord with braided edge for insertion
DMC Tapestry wool, 5 skeins of burgundy 7372
   1 skein each of

| | | | |
|---|---|---|---|
| white | | blue | 7302 |
| claret | 7115 | medium green | 7394 |
| light rose | 7132 | dark green | 7396 |
| pale pink | 7191 | gold | 7505 |
| dark rose | 7213 | light green | 7870 |

**1.** Following the chart, on which each square represents one stitch, embroider the design in tent stitch. Work the details first, then complete the panel by filling in the entire background with dark burgundy wool, using the basketweave tent stitch technique.

**2.** Spray the outside of the photo album lightly with glue and cover it with the piece of wadding. Trim the edges of the wadding level with the outer edges of the cover and set aside to dry.

**3.** Cut a piece of fabric 60 × 40 cm and place the opened album on the wrong side of it. Clip the material either side of the spine and trim off a small piece between the cuts, leaving approximately 1.5 cm to turn over into the spine. Glue the fabric in place all round the edges of the cover, clipping and mitering the corners, and taking care to leave enough 'give' in the cover to allow the album to close properly.

**4.** Cover the two rectangles of card with fabric, mitering the corners and glueing the turnings neatly in place on the back of each one. Glue these panels to the inside front and back covers of the photo album, covering the raw edges of the fabric.

**5.** Trim the canvas around the embroidery to a width of 2.5 cm on all sides. Fold the bare canvas to the back of the panel, mitering the corners, and pin in place. Pin the braided edge of the cording neatly around the edges, then stitch in place firmly. Join the ends of the cords together as invisibly as possible (see illustration). Remove all the pins.

**6.** Place the completed tapestry panel on the front of the photo album and pin in place. Using matching sewing cotton doubled, slip stitch it neatly to the upholstery fabric cover.

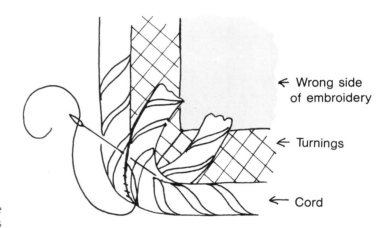

← Wrong side of embroidery

← Turnings

← Cord

## Key

| | |
|---|---|
| ≡≡≡ | White |
| ◣◣ | Claret 7115 |
| ⊞⊞ | Light rose 7132 |
| ⧄⧄ | Pale pink 7191 |
| ❷❷❷ | Dark rose 7213 |
| ⋀⋀⋀ | Blue 7302 |
| ⦀⦀ | Medium green 7394 |
| ■ | Dark green 7396 |
| ✕✕✕ | Gold 7505 |
| ∴∴∴ | Light green 7870 |
| ▨▨▨ | Burgundy 7372 |

**Working chart for photo album cover**

centre

centre

(each square on the chart equals one stitch)

# Bargello

Bargello is known by several other names, including flame stitch, Hungarian point and Florentine embroidery. It is a distinctive form of needlepoint embroidery in which patterns are built up using lines of straight stitches. Traditionally the colours shade from dark to light and back again in successive rows; often the effect is achieved through up to five shades of one colour. The easiest patterns are based on simple zigzag lines repeated over four threads from top to bottom of the canvas; once the first line is complete, the rest are worked identically, and the surface is very quickly filled. More complex patterns can be built up by reversing some rows or making shapes between them, which can either be filled with individual motifs or worked with more shaded rows of Bargello stitchery.

The name Bargello comes from a museum in the Italian town of Florence, which houses four chairs upholstered with this style of needlepoint and dating from the seventeenth century.

# 24. Blue spectacles case

*Materials*
canvas, 14 holes per 2.5 cm, 54 × 18 cm
blue felt 39 × 9.2 cm
25.5 cm strip plastic boning (used to stiffen strapless dresses)
Appleton's Crewel Wool,
   3 hanks of beige 961
   1 hank each of

| | | | |
|---|---|---|---|
| tan | 695 | dark rose | 755 |
| mid blue | 742 | silver grey | 987 |
| dark blue | 745 | | |

**1.** Mark the centre lines horizontally and vertically on the canvas. Measure up 17.5 cm from the centre point and start stitching the dark blue lines at the top of the centre square. Following the chart, on which each line represents one thread of the canvas, work the next 3 zigzag lines in dark blue.

**2.** Turn the canvas around and repeat step 1 at the opposite end, taking care that the centre stitches fall on the marked line to correspond with the first end.

**3.** Turn the canvas horizontally and work blue tent stitch lines between the zigzag patterns following the shades and sequence given in the chart. Fill in the remaining spaces with beige wool, using basketweave tent stitch.

**4.** Work the fill-in Bargello stitches at each end between the dark blue zigzag lines in dark rose and tan, following the chart.

**5.** Starting at the centre line with mid blue, work the satin stitch bands: the first stitch is taken over 3 threads of the canvas, the remainder over 4, with the row dropping 1 thread below the point of the top square. Complete the remaining horizontal rows, alternating silver grey with mid blue in lines of satin stitch over 4 threads. Turn the canvas around and repeat the pattern at the other end.

**6.** Trim the seam allowances of the canvas to 1 cm all round the edge of the stitching, and fold the bare canvas to the back of the work, leaving two unworked threads of canvas showing at either side. Centre the rectangle of felt over the back of the canvas with the top and bottom level with the second blue satin stitch bar from each end. Slip stitch the felt to the canvas along each side, using matching sewing cotton.

**7.** Turn the seam allowances on the ends of the canvas to the wrong side, then fold the last two satin stitch bars to the back, covering the edge of the felt. Slip stitch in place.

Cut 2 pieces of boning 8.5 cm long and slip one through each of these casings.

**8.** Fold the embroidered strip in half, wrong sides together, matching the patterns at the side edges, and stitch firmly together through the blank canvas threads at each edge, using binding stitch in dark blue crewel wool.

## Binding stitch

Turn the excess canvas to the back of the embroidery, leaving a bare thread at the edge of the work. Line up the holes along the edges of the two sections to be seamed together, then join in the thread at the point marked 1–2 on the diagram.

Follow the numbers given on the diagram to work the cross stitches, which form a strong and decorative edge with a plaited effect.

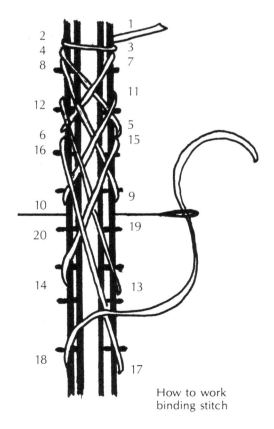

How to work
binding stitch

# Working chart for blue spectacles case

centre ▼

Key

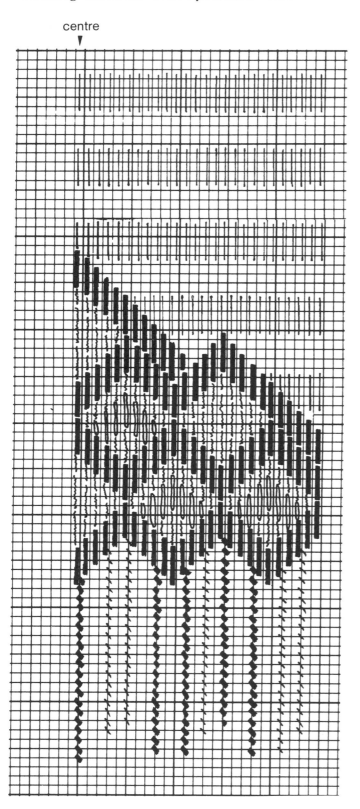

Tent stitch (dark blue 745

Straight stitch (dark blue 745)

Tent stitch (mid blue 742)

Straight stitch (mid blue 742)

Straight stitch (tan 695)

Straight stitch (dark rose 745)

(each line on the chart represents one thread of canvas)

# 25. Beige spectacles case

*Materials*
canvas, 14 holes per 2.5 cm, 54 × 18 cm
pink felt 50 × 10 cm
press stud 5 mm diameter
Appleton's Crewel Wool,
    2 hanks of light blue 561
    1 hank each of

| green | 353 | pale apricot | 702 |
| dark apricot | 621 | cream | 992 |
| old gold | 692 | | |

**1.** Starting 5 cm from the edge of the canvas at the point marked on Chart A, work the Bargello lines in light blue wool using 3 strands. Note that on the chart each line represents one thread of the canvas. Work the embroidery in a clockwise direction around the shape, following the chart, and finishing at the starting point.

**2.** Repeat step 1 five more times along the length of the canvas, so that there are 6 pairs of shapes outlined in blue altogether.

**3.** In the centre of each of the first 6 shapes, work the flower motif from the chart, using dark apricot for the petals and green for the stems and leaves. Turn the canvas around and work flower motifs in the remaining six shapes so that they point in the opposite direction from the first set. (When the case is made up, these will all finish with the stems pointing down to the bottom edge of the case.)

**4.** Work the background of each flower in basketweave tent stitch using light apricot wool.

**5.** Following Chart B, fill in the remaining shapes between the motifs with lines of stitches over 4 threads in the following colour sequence: gold, light apricot, white. Follow the blue lines under the first, second and third pairs of motifs, only filling in the top half of the shape under the third pair. Turn the canvas round and repeat the pattern at the opposite end of the case. Finish the top and bottom spaces above the end motifs with the bottom half of the pattern sequence.

**6.** Work the pattern from Chart C, starting at the centre point of the stitching at the end of the main panel. Using blue wool, work the outline of the flower motif and complete as before, then fill in the remaining stitches following the chart for the colours and their placement.

**7.** Cut the canvas with a margin of 1 cm on each straight side and fold the raw edges to the back of the embroidery, leaving one unworked thread at each side for binding stitch when making up the case.

**8.** Cut the felt to fit the back of the embroidery and pin, then slip stitch it in place around the three straight sides of the case.

**9.** Fold the canvas in two between the third and fourth pairs of flower motifs and align the patterns at the sides. Stitch together using three strands of gold wool to work binding stitch over the bare canvas threads at each side.

**10.** Trim the canvas around the edge of the flap to within 1 cm of the embroidery. Fold it to the back of the stitching and ease it to lie flat, leaving a small amount of canvas showing around the edges to take the binding stitch. Cut the felt to fit the flap and slip stitch it down to the turnings as neatly as possible. Complete the flap by working binding stitch in gold wool around the raw canvas at the edges to match the side seams of the case.

**11.** Sew half of the press stud to the underside of the flap and attach the corresponding half to the front of the case. Make a 5 cm long tassel from gold crewel wool and sew it to the centre of the curved edge of the flap.

# Working charts for beige spectacles case

**Chart A**

centre  Begin to stitch here

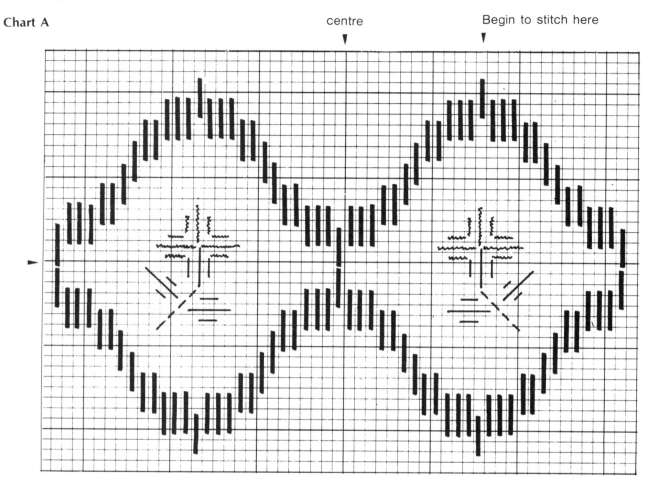

(each line on the chart represents one thread of the canvas)

**Key**

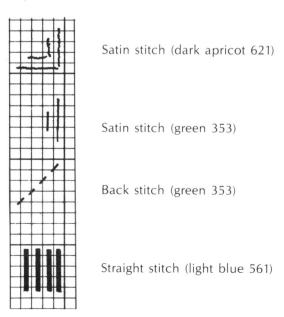

Satin stitch (dark apricot 621)

Satin stitch (green 353)

Back stitch (green 353)

Straight stitch (light blue 561)

## Chart B

### Key to charts B and C

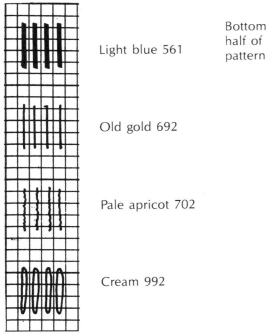

Light blue 561

Old gold 692

Pale apricot 702

Cream 992

Bottom half of pattern

Full Bargello pattern

Top half of pattern

centre

**Chart C, flap pattern**

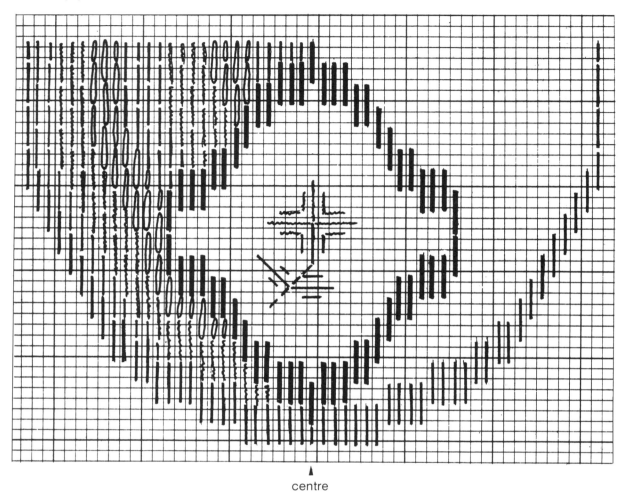

centre

# 26. Perforated paper Christmas card

*Materials*
red card blank 15.3 × 10.8 cm
white perforated paper 17 × 12 cm
DMC Stranded Cotton,

| | | | |
|---|---|---|---|
| white | | burgundy | 902 |
| green | 469 | dark pink | 3687 |

**1.** Following the chart on the next page, on which each square represents one stitch, embroider the design onto perforated paper. Start with the inner border and the side edges, then work the heart shapes. Embroider the grid pattern in back stitch last, stitching all the lines in one direction first, then working back over them the opposite way. Use 3 strands of cotton throughout.

**2.** Complete the centre panel with the holly pattern and lettering, using 6 strands of cotton to work the cross stitch berries and leaf tips. Use single lines of Milanese stitch for the main sections of the leaves, again using 6 strands of cotton, and use 3 strands for the back stitch lettering.

**3.** Cut away the excess paper around the outer edges of the embroidery, leaving a 2 mm margin. Use sharp pointed embroidery scissors for best results.

**4.** Glue the inside flap of the card into place, then spread glue lightly over the back of the embroidery and press it onto the front of the card.

## Working chart for perforated paper Christmas card

(each square on the chart represents one stitch)

centre

## Key

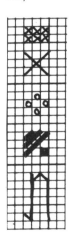

Cross stitch (white))

Back stitch (white)

Cross stitch (dark pink 3687)

Milanese stitch (green 469)
Cross stitch (green 469)

Back stitch (burgundy 902)

# 27. Large Christmas card

*Materials*
red card blank 20.5 × 15.2 cm
50 cm silver lace, 20 mm wide
canvas, 14 holes per 2.5 cm, 15 cm square
DMC Medici Crewel Wool, green 8403
Ribbon Floss, silver
   iridescent pearl
Watercolour Cotton by Caron, Autumn Leaves

**1.** Following the chart on the next page, on which each line represents one thread of the canvas, start at the centre of the canvas and embroider a diamond eyelet stitch over 4 threads using silver ribbon floss.

**2.** Continue stitching use the Watercolour Cotton. Work. from the centre outwards and back again on each shape to keep the colours flowing on from one to another.

**3.** Work the centre square in doubled iridescent pearl ribbon floss, then the 4 double cross stitches in silver. Finally, fill in the entire background area with basketweave tent stitch using 3 strands of Medici crewel wool.

**4.** Cut the canvas between the third and fourth threads beyond the stitching all round the square. Cover the back lightly with glue and position the shape on the front of the folded card. Cover the raw edges of the canvas by glueing on silver lace edging, mitering the corners neatly and securing them in position with a dab of glue underneath.

*Note* This type of card can be easily made using a sheet of red card 30.5 × 20.5 cm. Mark the centres of the long sides and score a line between them using a point of your scissors and a metal-edged ruler. Fold on the scored line. Lettering can be added using rubber stamps, calligraphy, transfers, or any other suitable technique. Experiment with the position of the embroidery before glueing it in place.

# Working chart for large Christmas card

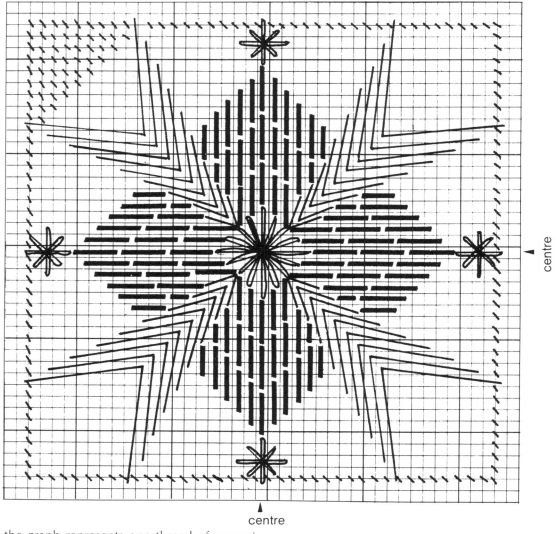

centre

centre

(each line on the graph represents one thread of canvas)

## Key

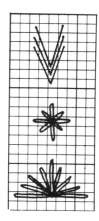

Straight stitch (Watercolour Cotton)

Double cross stitch (silver ribbon floss)

Diamond eyelet stitch (silver ribbon floss)

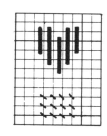

Satin stitch (iridescent pearl ribbon floss)

Tent stitch (Medici Crewel Wool, green)

# 28. Christmas cornucopia

*Materials*
canvas, 12 threads per 2.5 cm, 30 cm square
DMC Tapestry wool, 3 skeins of white
Appleton's Crewel Wool, green 396
DMC Pearl Cotton No. 3,
   claret          902              pink         3687
silver Ribbon Floss
37 X 2 mm pearl beads
random-dyed crewel wool, pink shades
50 cm silver lace, 22 mm wide
30 cm silver braid, 5 mm wide
pink felt 20 cm square

1. Measure 13 cm down from the top of the canvas, along the centre line, to establish the centre of the heart and bow design. Following the chart on page 105, on which each line represents one thread of the canvas, embroider the bow in tent stitch with a satin stitch knot, using doubled strands of pearl cotton. Work the date in pearl beads using a fine beading needle with doubled white sewing cotton, then fill in the background heart in tent stitch using three strands of the variegated pink wool.

2. Using a single strand of silver ribbon floss, work the lace-effect edging around the heart in straight stitches between the marked dots, following the chart.

3. Work a line of chain stitch around the heart shape in silver, keeping to the centre of the shaded area shown on the chart. Using 3 strands of green crewel wool, work rows of back stitch either side of the chain stitch to cover the shaded area entirely.

4. Complete the shapes of the edging by filling in the triangles with straight stitches from each outer point to the edge of the shaded area.

5. Trace the template for the curve from page 102 and cut out. Position the straight edge along the row of stitches between the base of the bow and the top of the numbers with the vertical line matching the centre of the canvas. Use a fade-out pen to draw along the curved edge onto the canvas. Check that the curve finishes at the same thread of canvas on each side of the motif.

6. Using white tapestry wool, work a diagonal line of tent stitch from each end of the curved line to meet at the centre line of the canvas, approximately 8.5 cm below the bottom two pink tent stitches in the heart motif. Note that the two lines will meet each other with two stitches together on the same line.

7. Starting at the lowest point, fill in the entire background area between the tent stitched diagonals and the top curve of the design with Parisian stitch, using white tapestry wool.

8. Trim the canvas all round the embroidery to 1 cm in width, and turn the raw edges to the wrong side as evenly as possible. Cut a piece of pink felt to exactly the same size as the embroidered area and slip stitch it to the back of the work using matching sewing cotton.

9. Fold the embroidery with wrong sides together and join the short edges using binding stitch with white wool. Gather the straight edge of the silver lace to fit around the open end of the cone, allowing 2 cm of overlap, and seam the ends together. Sew the lace to the outside of the top of the cone with small stitches using white sewing cotton.

10. Stitch each end of the silver braid to the inside of the cone shape at the top, halfway between the back seam and the centre of the motif.

*Note* To change the date on the motif, refer to the lettering charts given for the Victorian beaded pincushions and substitute the numbers required.

Actual size template for top curve

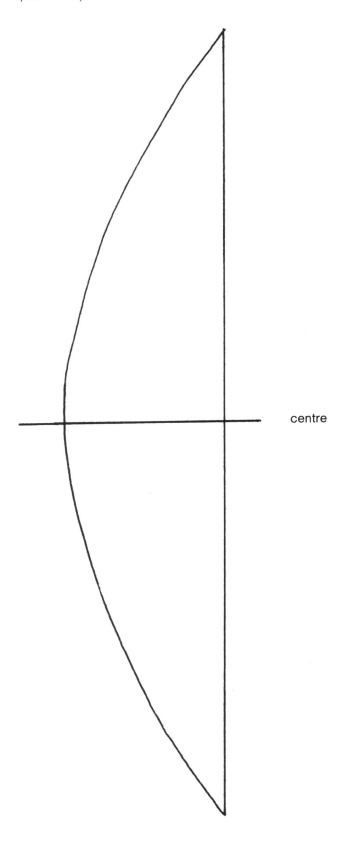

centre

Projects 29, 30 and 31: Christmas tree decorations

Project 32: Notebook cover

# Working chart for Christmas cornucopia

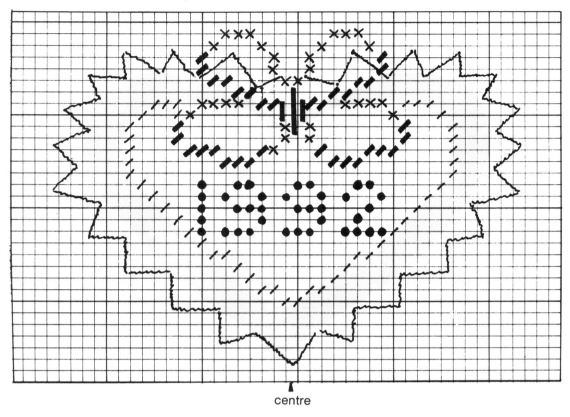

centre

(each line on the graph equals one thread of canvas)

## Key

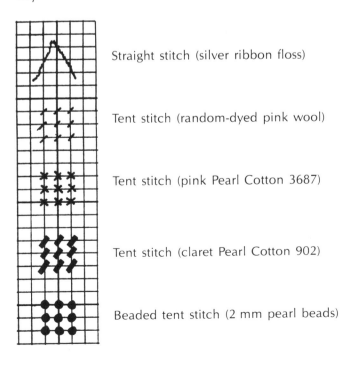

Straight stitch (silver ribbon floss)

Tent stitch (random-dyed pink wool)

Tent stitch (pink Pearl Cotton 3687)

Tent stitch (claret Pearl Cotton 902)

Beaded tent stitch (2 mm pearl beads)

# 29. Fan tree decoration

## Materials

Twilleys' Gold Dust, silver
DMC Pearl Cotton No. 3,
    white                      burgundy     902
12 cm silver lace 20 mm wide
silver Ribbon Floss
25 cm white ribbon 3 mm wide
silver card, paper or leather 4 cm square
plastic canvas circle 7.5 cm diameter

**1.** Carefully cut the quarter circle out of the plastic canvas as shown in the diagram.

**2.** Following the chart, work rows of cross stitches alternating with Gobelin stitches in the colours indicated, starting with bar 2 and ending on bar 7. Use doubled lengths of thread throughout.

**3.** Using white pearl cotton as a single strand, join the thread to the back of the embroidery near to the point of the fan and oversew the edges up the side, across bar 8 using 2 Gobelin stitches in each hole, and down the other side. Sew across bar 1 in Gobelin stitch and oversew around the edge of the base triangle before finishing off the thread securely.

**4.** Work a row of buttonhole stitch in doubled ribbon floss across the top bar of the canvas to complete the embroidery.

**5.** Turn the raw edges of the lace to the wrong side and glue in place, then gently gather the lace and glue it to the back of the embroidery along the top edge.

**6.** Fold the narrow white ribbon in half and glue the ends to the back of the fan shape, leaving a loop approximately 9 cm long for hanging. Cover the back of the embroidery with a piece of silver paper cut to shape and glued in place.

**7.** Use Gold Dust thread to make a 5 cm long tassel and sew it to the bottom triangle so that it hangs down beneath the fan.

## Key

| Symbol | No. | Description |
|---|---|---|
| ᙢ | 9 | Buttonhole (silver ribbon floss) |
| ▮▮▮ | 8 | Gobelin stitch (white Pearl Cotton) |
| ✕ | 7 | Cross stitch (silver ribbon floss) |
| ✕ | 6 | Cross stitch (silver ribbon floss) |
| ✸ |  | Cross stitch (burgundy Pearl Cotton) |
| ◑◑ | 5 | Gobelin stitch (burgundy Pearl Cotton) |
| ✕ | 4 | Cross stitch (silver ribbon floss) |
| ✸ |  | Cross stitch (burgundy Pearl Cotton) |
| ❘❘❘ | 3 | Gobelin stitch (silver ribbon floss) |
| ✕ | 2 | Cross stitch (silver ribbon floss) |
| ▮▮▮ | 1 | Gobelin stitch (white Pearl Cotton) |

**Cutting diagram for plastic canvas fan decoration**

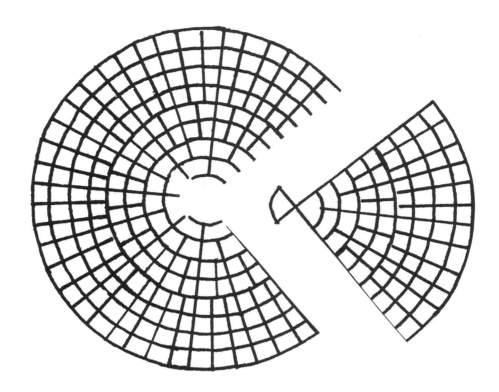

**Working chart for fan tree decoration**

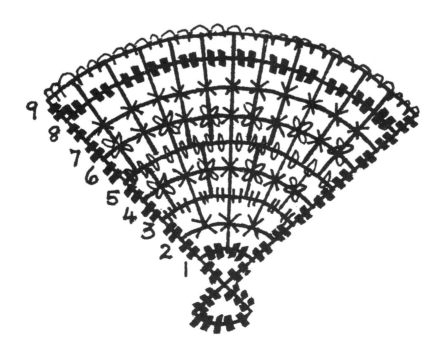

# 30. Heart-shaped tree decoration

## Materials

plastic canvas heart shape, 9 cm wide
1 m silver lace, 20 mm wide
50 cm white satin ribbon, 3 mm wide
Silver Ribbon Floss
DMC Pearl cotton No. 3,
    white                    pink        3687

**1.** Following the chart, embroider the heart shape using threads and stitches as shown. Use doubled strands of ribbon floss and a single thickness of Pearl Cotton No. 3.
**2.** Gather the lace and join the ends together neatly. Place the seam at the centre top of the heart, and using white sewing cotton slip stitch the edge of the lace to the buttonhole-stitched edge of the heart.
**3.** Fold the length of white ribbon in half and make an overhand knot leaving a 12 cm long loop. Sew the knot at the centre top of the heart and tie the ends of the ribbon in a bow, catching it in place with a few small stitches.

## Working chart for plastic canvas heart decoration

(each dot (•) on the pattern is one hole of the canvas)

### Key

Buttonhole stitch (silver ribbon floss)

Chain stitch (pink Pearl Cotton)

Back stitch (white Pearl Cotton)

Back stitch (silver ribbon floss)

Diamond eyelet (white Pearl Cotton)

Upright cross (silver ribbon floss)

Chain stitch (white Pearl Cotton)

Straight stitch (silver ribbon floss)

# 31. Small basket tree decoration

*Materials*
plastic canvas circle, 7.5 cm diameter
iridescent pearl Ribbon Floss
DMC Pearl Cotton No. 3,
   green          987           pink          3687
50 cm silver lace, 20 mm wide
white felt, 7.5 cm diameter circle
1 metal macrame ring, 30 mm diameter
plastic canvas, 10 holes per 2.5 cm, 15 × 1 cm

**1.** Lightly glue the metal ring to the centre of the plastic canvas circle so that it covers bar 3 as shown in Chart A on the next page. Using green pearl cotton doubled, oversew the ring to the canvas around bar 3, covering the ring as neatly and smoothly as possible.
**2.** Work Rhodes stitch across the central circle inside the ring to cover the canvas completely, and fasten off the thread securely.
**3.** Using a double strand of pearlised ribbon floss, work back stitch over the exposed spokes of the canvas next to the ring, covering them completely.
**4.** Using green pearl cotton as a single thread, work cross stitch along the complete spokes as shown in Chart B on page 111.

**5.** Work groups of 7 cross stitches with doubled pink pearl cotton in the large spaces as shown on the chart.
**6.** Work tent and Gobelin stitches in ribbon floss around each pink triangle as shown, then fill in the remaining smaller triangles of the design with a cross stitch over bar 4 and straight stitches as shown.
**7.** Finish the edge of the circle by oversewing it with a single strand of green pearl cotton.
**8.** Make the handle by working a row of cross stitch in doubled ribbon floss over 2 holes along the centre of the strip. Oversew the outer edges with a single thread of green pearl cotton.
**9.** Sew each end of the handle to the wrong side of the circle behind opposite pink triangle motifs. Run a thread from each side through the threads covering the base and pull tightly to hold the sides inwards, then fasten off securely.
**10.** Gather the lace edging and join the ends together as invisibly as possible. Glue the lace around the edge of the basket on the inside. Line the basket with the circle of white felt, covering all the raw edges and threads.

# Working charts for Christmas basket

### Chart A

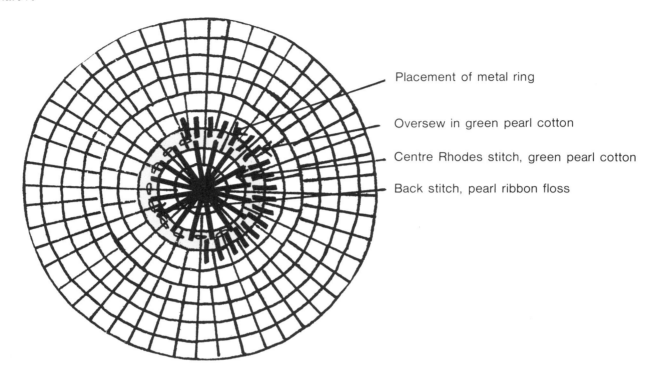

Placement of metal ring

Oversew in green pearl cotton

Centre Rhodes stitch, green pearl cotton

Back stitch, pearl ribbon floss

### Rhodes stitch detail

Work following the number sequence, coming up in odd-numbered holes, and going down through those with even numbers.

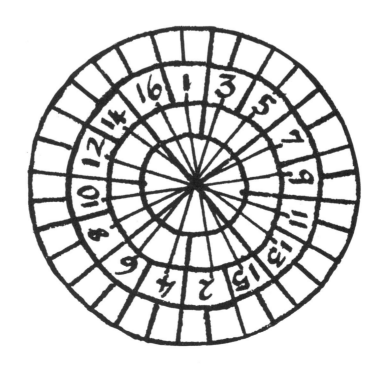

**Chart B**

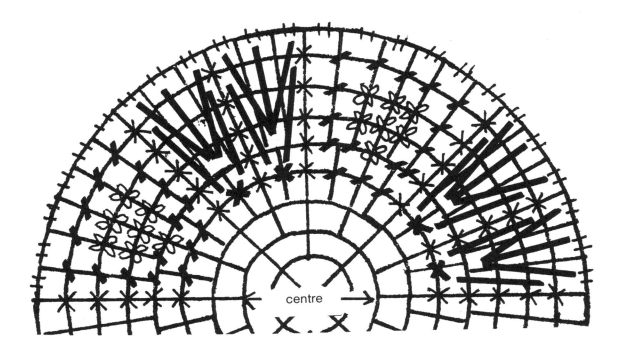

centre →

X . X

**Key**

X      Cross stitch (green pearl cotton)

III      Oversewn edge (green pearl cotton)

⊗      Cross stitch (pink pearl cotton)

✘      Cross stitch (iridescent pearl ribbon floss)

✎      Tent stitch (iridescent pearl ribbon floss)

➤      Straight stitch (iridescent pearl ribbon floss)

# 32. Notebook cover

## Materials

canvas, 14 holes per 2.5 cm, 45 × 30 cm
Appleton's Crewel Wools, 1 hank each of

| | | | |
|---|---|---|---|
| beige | 201 | dark red | 505 |
| tan | 303 | dark green | 546 |
| dark brown | 304 | pale pink | 752 |
| very dark brown | 305 | mid pink | 753 |
| light green | 401 | dark rose | 755 |
| yellow | 472 | off white | 991 |

8 hanks of dark blue 566
blue felt 52.5 × 18.5 cm
iron-on heavyweight interfacing 18 × 23 cm
notebook 17 × 13 cm, approximately 2 cm thick

**1.** Measure a point 10 cm from one long edge of the canvas and 9.5 cm from the short side, and start stitching with the yellow cross stitch, following Chart A, on which each square represents one stitch. Complete the tent stitch motifs for the front and spine, including the border, using colours as shown. Work all five of the yellow cross stitch flower centres from this chart.

**2.** Changing to Chart B, on which each line represents one thread of the canvas, work the flower motifs around the yellow cross stitches, using the larger one in the centre of the design, and repeating the small one in each corner.

**3.** Fill in the entire background area with dark blue basketweave tent stitch.

**4.** Work the back panel of the cover in triple brick stitch to measure 13.5 × 18.5 cm.

**5.** Trim the canvas to 2.5 cm all round the edge of the stitching and fold the turnings to the wrong side. Cut the interfacing in half to measure 18 × 11.5 cm and iron one piece onto each end of the felt strip.

**6.** Fold over the ends of the felt with the interfacing on the inside, and centre the strip on top of the wrong side of the embroidery. Pin in place all round the edges, trimming to fit if necessary. The interfaced ends form pockets into which the notebook will be slipped.

**7.** Oversew the felt neatly to the canvas all around the edge of the embroidery. Bend the covers of the notebook back and slip them into the pockets of the cover, then ease the book closed, stretching the cover into place.

*Note*  Because book sizes can vary considerably, check the measurements before making this cover. The pattern can be enlarged or reduced slightly by adding or subtracting rows in the outer tent-stitch borders, keeping the colours in sequence. A thinner book can have the spine panel omitted altogether, or replaced with tent stitch in either the plain background blue or the border pattern in shades of browns.

**Key**

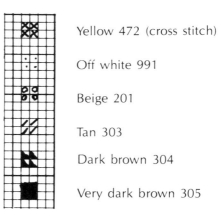

Yellow 472 (cross stitch)

Off white 991

Beige 201

Tan 303

Dark brown 304

Very dark brown 305

# Working chart for notebook cover

**Chart A**

(each square on the graph represents one stitch)

**Chart B**

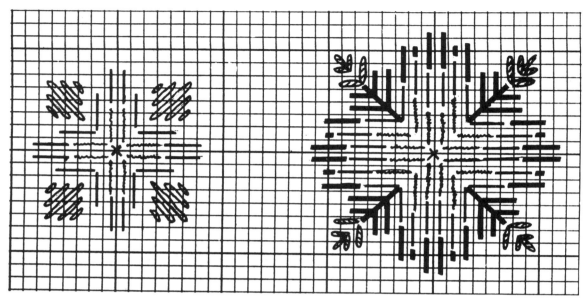

(each line on the chart represents one thread of canvas)

**Key**

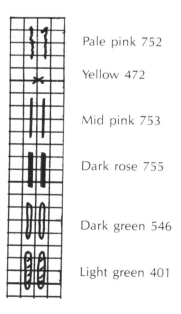

Pale pink 752

Yellow 472

Mid pink 753

Dark rose 755

Dark green 546

Light green 401

# Conversion chart:
# Appleton's Crewel Wool
# to DMC Tapestry Wool

There is often no direct-match in the shades produced by the two companies, so numbers given in brackets ( ) in the following chart are my suggestions for an alternative.

| Appleton's Crewel Wool | DMC Tapestry Wool | Appleton's Crewel Wool | DMC Tapestry Wool |
|---|---|---|---|
| 201 | 7271 | 701 | 7141 |
| 245 | 7393 | 702 | 7451 |
| 256 | 7988 | 741 | (7799) |
| 292 | 7870 | 742 | 7799 |
| 303 | 7845 | 745 | (7798) |
| 304 | 7479 | 751 | 7132 |
| 305 | 7479 | 752 | 7132 |
| 341 | (7870) | 753 | 7193 |
| 351 | 7402 | 755 | 7195 |
| 353 | 7424 | 821 | 7798 |
| 396 | 7408 | 841 | 7371 |
| 401 | (7384) | 873 | (7400) |
| 447 | 7606 | 875 | (7715) |
| 461 | (7799) | 877 | 7170 |
| 472 | 7472 | 941 | 7424 |
| 505 | 7198 | 944 | 7204 |
| 544 | 7769 | 948 | (7108) |
| 546 | 7988 | 961 | 7282 |
| 566 | 7650 | 987 | 7300 |
| 621 | 7192 | 991 | White |
| 692 | 7493 | 992 | Ecru |
| 695 | 7505 | 993 | Black |

# Adapting designs

The charted designs can be worked on any size canvas; using a fabric with fewer holes per 2.5 cm will enlarge the finished pattern, and may require an extra strand of crewel wool in order to make the stitches cover the canvas correctly. Conversely, a finer canvas will require thinner threads and produce a smaller finished item.

If the colours of a project do not suit your tastes, it is easy to substitute some which are more suitable. Check the list of colours required for the project and note how many shades of the main colours are required, then substitute the same number of shades in your chosen colour. You may also have to alter the other colours of the project slightly; place all the colours together with your own selection and check that they go together well; if one is wrong, try a slightly different shade from the original. If in doubt, call for a second opinion; it is amazing how good the judgment of family members and friends who profess to know nothing about such things can be. (I write from experience!)

The designs are also very adaptable. An individual motif such as that on the needlework set could be worked as a repeat pattern to make a cushion; the motif on the apple blossom cushion could be worked singly on a box lid or pincushion; the panel of the edelweiss cushion looks good framed and hung on the wall. Different borders can be substituted for the given ones, although a bit of basic arithmetic may be necessary to make sure that they will fit. All the scraps of canvas left over from projects can be used to experiment with ideas; mount the best in cards or make them up into small gift items, or simply file them away for future reference. A stamp dealer can supply you with some plastic album pages in standard sizes which are just right for this sort of thing; they are designed to hold complete stamped envelopes. These little projects can be worked without frames, and can be easily carried around with you to ease the boredom of long journeys or fill the time spent in professionals' waiting rooms.

# Caring for needlepoint

Because canvas is stiffened with size, getting it wet makes it limp, so finished needlepoint pieces should not be washed. Mounted panels and upholstery in wool on canvas respond well to a clean with a vacuum cleaner using the upholstery attachment. Do this every few weeks. Sponge stains out gently with mild soap and water; an upholstery stainguard spray treatment can be used when the project is finished, but it is a good idea to test it out on a sample or an inconspicuous spot first, just to make sure that there are no problems with it.

Plastic canvas items are washable, even when stitched in wool, but linings must be removed first. Perforated paper cannot be cleaned at all, and it is for this reason that most of the projects which use it are protected with glass.

# List of suppliers

DMC Needlecraft Pty Ltd
PO Box 317
Earlwood NSW 2206

Tapestry Wool
Medici Wool
Stranded Cotton
Pearl Cotton
Canvases

DMC products are widely available in department stores and craft shops throughout Australia.

Rannelle Designs
6 Tebera Street
Westlake Qld 4074
Mail order service

Greetings card blanks

Swanland Crafts
PO Box
Belmont WA 6104
Mail order service

Bookmark cards

D.D. Creative Crafts
PO Box 565
Ringwood Vic 3134
Wholesale distributors

Perforated paper

Ireland Needlecraft
4, 2-4 Keppel Drive
Hallam Vic 3803
Wholesale distributor

Famecraft brooch and
pendant findings
DMC distributor

Rajmahal Art Imports
Fosterville Road
Bagshot East Vic 3551
Mail order service

Pure silk and
metallic threads

In Vogue Decor
4 University Place
Clayton Vic 3168

Space dyed crewel wools

Down Under Australia
33 Peacock Street
Seaforth NSW 2092
Mail order

Watercolour threads
Frames and accessories

The Tapestry Guild
PO Box 102
Baulkham Hills NSW 2153
Mail order

Canvas work supplies

Anne's Glory Box
60 Beaumont Street
Hamilton
Newcastle NSW 2303
Mail order

General sewing and crafts

The Silver Thimble
339 Rokeby Road
Subiaco WA 6008
Mail order

Appleton's Crewel Wool
DMC Threads
Canvas and equipment
Plastic canvas
Perforated paper

Needle Art & Wools
7a Cinema City Arcade
Hay Street
Perth WA 6000
Mail order

Appleton's Crewel Wool
DMC Threads
Canvas and equipment
Silk gauze

Creative Bead Imports
Fremantle Crafts and
Supplies
Delicate Stitches
225 South Terrace
South Fremantle WA 6162
Mail order

Beads
Jewellery findings
Appleton's Crewel Wool
DMC Threads
Canvas and equipment
Watercolour threads

Gilbert Bridal Floral &
Handcraft
306 Murray Street
Perth WA 6000
Mail order

DMC Threads
Canvas and frames
Plastic canvas
Ribbon Floss
Beads
Jewellery findings

W.H.J. Hardie & Co.
68 King Street
Perth WA 6000
Mail order

Upholstery supplies
Linen thread
Cords and braids

P.L. Stonewall & Co.
52 Erskine Street
Sydney NSW 2000

Importers and agents for
Appleton's Crewel Wools

Clifton H. Joseph
391 Little Lonsdale Street
Melbourne Vic 3000

Importers and agents for
Appleton's Crewel Wools

# Index